Constructive Feedback

Learning the Art

The Story of Oliver and Taylor

Brent Kilbourn

BROOKLINE
BOOKS

The Ontario Institute for Studies in Education has three prime functions: to conduct programs of graduate study in education, to undertake research in education, and to assist in the implementation of the findings of educational studies. The Institute is a college chartered by an Act of the Ontario Legislature in 1965. It is affiliated with the University of Toronto for graduate studies purposes.

The publications program of the Institute has been established to make available information and materials arising from studies in education, to foster the spirit of critical inquiry, and to provide a forum for the exchange of ideas about education. The opinions expressed should be viewed as those of the contributors.

©The Ontario Institute for Studies in Educaiton 1990
252 Bloor Street West
Toronto, Ontario
M5S 1V5

Canadian Cataloguing in Publication Data
Kilbourn, Brent, 1942-
  Constructive feedback

(Monograph series ; 24)
Includes bibliographical references.
ISBN 0-7744-0351-9

1. Teaching — Evaluation — Case studies.
2. Educational evaluation — Case studies.
3. Feedback (Psychology) — Case studies. I. Title.
II. Series: Monograph series (Ontario Institute
for Studies in Education) ; 24.

LB1731.K54 1990   371.1'44   C90-093803-X

Library of Congress Cataloging-in-Publication Data
Kilbourn, Brent.
  Constructive feedback : learning the art / by Brent Kilbourn.
     p.   cm.
  Includes bibliographical references.
  ISBN 0-914797-78-6 (paper)
  1. Curriculum planning. 2. Feedback (Psychology) 3. Teaching.
I. Title.
LB2806.15.K55 1990   90-2271
375'.001--dc20   CIP

ISBN 0-7744-0351-9   Printed in Canada

1 2 3 4 5 HPL 49 39 29 19 09

Contents

Acknowledgments

It is an unfortunate ethical artifact of case study research that the very people who have given so much cannot be mentioned by their real names. Nevertheless, I want to thank Oliver and Taylor for making this study possible. Their courage in allowing their work to be documented has gained my respect and admiration. I hope that the account adequately reflects their dedication and expertise.

I also want to thank those who gave me constructive feedback during the development of this case: Agostino Tobia, Alex Norrie, Allan MacKinnon, Ann Nicholson, Anne Webb, Art Geddis, Austin Hart, Barb Kilbourn, Bernie Gelfand, Beverley Madigan, Bill Louden, Bob LaRose, Brendan Rogers, Brian Beth, Carol Mullen, Catherine Giovinazzo, Catherine Keating, Cheri Hernandez, Clarice Steers, Colin Armstrong, Connie Heimbecker, David Coe, Dennis Tate, Diane Titus, Donald Schön, Donna Ward, Doug Roberts, Ellen Regan, Frances Tolnai, Fred Stocovaz, Geoff Roberts, Gila Strauch, Harjit Dhillon, Harvey Starkman, Hugh Oliver, Irene Ross, Jane Michaud, Jesse Lees, Jim Butler, Jim Gaskell, Jim Hall, Jim Howes, Joanne Johnson, Joe Kenny, Joe Parchelo, John Bertram, John McCulloch, John Wallace, Juanita Neal, Judith Laskin, Judy Youell, Karen Murray, Karen Timson, Laird Orr, Margaret Joyce, Marguerite Allen, Mich Bondy, Michael Connelly, Monique Pigeon-Abolins, Naomi Norquay, Nick Bruzzese, Oliver, Patrick Allen, Rick Lloyd, Roger Simon, Ruth Spearing, Sandy McNabb, Skip Hills, Steven Bland, Taylor, Theresa George, Theresa Hyland, Thi-Anh Huynh, Tom Joyce, Tom McCaul, Tom Osler, Wendy Wright, and Ziona Greisman.

This work was funded by the Social Science and Humanities Research Council of Canada. Grant #410-83-1232.

B.K.

Notes to the Reader

** This book is for anyone interested in constructive feedback as a form of professional development. It is a book about curriculum development and implementation, teaching, and feedback. It should be of interest to teachers, consultants, department heads, administrators, and some academics.

** The book's basic premise is that if we are really serious about the process of feedback then at some point we must move from rhetoric to a reflective inquiry of actual cases — to issues about the process that emerge from real feedback situations and which help us think about our own situations.

** There are many voices in this case: the teacher, the students, the observer (indicated by T, S, and O respectively in the dialogue), the subject matter, the administrator, the researcher. You may identify or sympathize with some voices more than others, but the important point is that in an actual situation each wants to be heard and all must be considered in the feedback process.

** This is not a manual or a how-to-do-it book even though its contents may be informative in these ways. You will not find summaries or exhortations about, for example, "Steps that must be taken if feedback is to be truly collegial," as these are more than adequately treated in different kinds of books from this one. *This is a book that will work best if actively discussed.* It is a book to be read with a colleague or in a group or, if alone, with internal dialogue. Discussions should be aimed at an active inquiry about the case along with reflections on your own situation.

** The sections prior to Day 1 set the context, but you may wish occasionally to turn to the last section, "Questions and Responses," which contains selected questions from the more than seventy readers of earlier drafts of the case. A list of these questions is on pages 109-110.

Introducing Constructive Feedback

In this case study the generic term "feedback" is used to indicate any process in which one professional comments on another's practice (usually) based on observation and aimed at professional development rather than performance evaluation. Constructive feedback is one way that practitioners learn their work and develop professionally. Within the teaching profession the attitude toward feedback is mixed. Practitioners seldom question the potential of constructive feedback for contributing to professional growth and the improvement of teaching. But they do have concerns about the time it takes to engage the process seriously, the circumstances within which it is done, and the implications for their professional autonomy. Their concerns provoke the question, *What makes feedback constructive?*

The question has no quick answer. Although this case study contains exemplary instances of constructive feedback, it is not a model. And, although there are instances of feedback included which could merit rethinking, it is also not put forward as an example of bad practice. Rather, the case is an example which is detailed enough to clearly illustrate the complexities of the feedback process, and to show that real cases are neither all good nor all bad. By documenting the intricacies of sustained feedback I hope to show its potential and, perhaps more important, the sense in which constructive, collegial feedback in teaching is a *learned art*. It requires practice, patience, and the willingness to study and reflect.

The complexities of feedback are especially important considering the renewed interest in feedback as a component of pre-service and in-service teacher education.[1] Rhetoric about the value of feedback for professional development is common. Coaching, mentoring, peer coaching, collegial feedback, supervision for growth, and clinical supervision are all processes which involve settings in which feedback is commonly part of the interaction between practitioners. Whatever the particular slant of such processes (and there are important differences) they are all aimed at *professional development* rather than evaluation, and their rhetoric is intended to convey a more sensitive and effective kind of interaction than in an earlier time of School Inspectors. The expectation is that feedback will be professionally rewarding, and that it will improve teaching. The conviction is that it is needed.

But teachers are seldom observed and given systematic feedback on a regular basis even by those who have the authority and responsibility (if not the time) to do so, let alone by their own colleagues who would be best informed about the nature of classroom life. Consequently, there are very few case histories about the feedback process in the literature or in the oral history of the professional culture. Timely though the calls for feedback might be, it is not an easy process, and few teachers have had any sustained experience with it.

Constructive feedback in teaching is a complicated process; it calls for constant attention to details and context, and for active inquiry *in practice* as well as reflection on reconstructed accounts of practice. An underlying argument of this case study is that careful consideration of real cases can help bring our images of practice and our actual practice closer together. It is through the consideration of instances of practice, informed by our theoretical notions of what that practice should be like, that we can begin to understand our own practice and improve it. At the same time we develop more adequate and satisfying theoretical images of what that practice should be. The function of this case, then, is to provide an instance of the feedback process which is rich enough in context and detail to allow those interested in feedback to construct an anatomy of the process, question assumptions and practices, imagine alternatives, and think about their own practice.

The plan of the book

This book is essentially a contextual account of interaction. As with any account that tries to honour the context of events, there is a question of how much should be said before the reader gets to the heart of the matter. The next three sections ("Background," "A Point of View on Feedback," and "Foreground") set the broad context for reflecting on two teachers' work together. The account proper, the heart of the matter, begins with "Day 1" on page 19 and continues through "Day 13." The account is an interpretive documentation of the feedback process between a teacher (Taylor) and his colleague who was his department head (Oliver).[2] The account covers nearly two weeks of teaching a unit on cancer and cell biology to adolescent science students. The discussion of each day's events is in three parts (identified as "Class," "Conference," and "Considerations") as follows:

• A brief description of Taylor's class.

• A detailed description of Oliver and Taylor's conversation about class.

• Considerations about Oliver and Taylor's interaction and, more generally, about the entire feedback process.

Following the account of Oliver and Taylor's work together is a section called "Reflections" in which I consider the case as a whole, drawing out some of the strands that run through it. The last section, "Questions and Responses," is an attempt to address readers' comments but also, conveniently, serves as a vehicle for emphasizing certain issues in the account itself. These last two sections allow me, on the one hand, to show what sense I have made of the feedback process and, on the other, to reflect more generally on the work as a case study.

---

1. For instance, in southern Ontario a number of school boards have instituted in-service programs based on some form of feedback, and one part of the Learning Consortium at the Faculty of Education University of Toronto is based on "mentoring" as the vehicle for pre-service training.

2. B. Kilbourn and D. A. Roberts, *Science, Society, and the Non-Academic Student: Phase II, Final Report* (Ottawa: Social Sciences and Humanities Research Council, 1987). The present case was one of four in a project aimed at documenting and discussing the nature of observation and feedback to teachers of adolescent science students in general-level courses. The broad goals of the project were to contribute to an understanding of what it means to teach this group of students and to an understanding of the feedback process itself.

Background

This case study had its origins with a group of science teachers who, because of their concern about the lack of appropriate curriculum materials for use in general-level courses, began to design science units which specifically attended to some of the qualities of this level of learners.[1] These units had several distinctive features. Each had a theme which continued for the duration of the unit, and all of the lessons, readings, and activities were integrated with this central theme. The intent was to provide students with coherent experiences rather than piecemeal information. The unit materials also contained numerous activities which were intended to engage students as active rather than passive learners, and which, at the same time, had intellectual substance.

The units also all had a science-and-society emphasis; each in different ways emphasized the relationship between science and broader social concerns.[2] For example, discussion of the imminent extinction of some species of whales was used to focus on ecological issues. Another issue used was the problem of water pollution and the available techniques for water treatment. The unit used in this case study concerns the importance of cell biology for understanding, diagnosing, and treating cancer. The science-society emphasis of these units served both ideological and motivational purposes: teachers wanted to address broader social issues related to science, and they thought that such an emphasis would be genuinely more interesting to students who normally do not relate well to the fact-learning orientation of much standard "academic" teaching.

In spite of the hard work of many people, some of the units received limited use after their initial development. It was a familiar story — a flurry of summer writing which produced a first draft and then, the shelf. It must be recognized that curriculum development is often a slow process: good final drafts usually only come from successive, documented field trials. This process is demanding and not one that a teacher is eager to add to an already full schedule unless she or he has some indication that the new materials "work."

The question of whether or not a unit "works" is difficult because of the integrated nature of teaching and materials. A unit of material is only as good as the teaching, and the quality of the teaching is often compromised by the unavailability and poor quality of curriculum materials (which provided the impetus for the development of the units in the first place). Preliminary observations of some of the draft units suggested that they might be difficult to use. This gave rise to a project in which implementation was looked at more systematically.[3]

Seven different cases of the implementation of various trial versions of the units were studied. Two impressions which had considerable impact on the project team (consisting of practicing and non-practicing teachers) emerged from observing and documenting the implementation process of each unit. The first was the recognition of how difficult and time-consuming it was for teachers to work with material that was "activity" based. The activities in the units not only called for a new style of interaction (in many cases) between students and teachers, but also involved the frustrating and lengthy task of acquiring and setting up materials. Once routines and mechanisms are in place, of course, it requires much less energy and concentration to teach a unit another time, but the first time is a chore.

The second realization was that the implementation of new materials presented in situation ripe for constructive feedback and concrete assistance from a colleague. Considering the reluctance of teachers to teach new, untested units of material, it seemed that this was a time when a teacher could really benefit from the helping hand of an informed colleague, someone who could be supportive in a variety of ways and who could usefully document the implementation process at critical points. In the present case, Taylor decided to use one of the trial units and Oliver, his department head, agreed to give him feedback and support.

---

1. This work was done in Ontario where courses are offered at three levels of difficulty (basic, general, and advanced). Many educators, parents, and students are offended by labelling students, hence talk about general-level *students* is discouraged in favour of general-level *courses* which students opt to take. Basic-level courses emphasize life skills. General-level courses are wide ranging but are intended to prepare students for employment or entry into Colleges of Applied Arts and Technology. Advanced-level courses focus on academic skills and prepare students for entry to university. In the dialogue of this case study, when the term "general" refers to a student it is being used to indicate a student who is enrolled in general-level courses.

2. For a discussion of the concept of "curriculum emphasis" and the idea of theme or story-line in curriculum materials development, see: Douglas A. Roberts, "Developing the Concept of 'Curriculum Emphasis' in Science Education," *Science Education* 66(2) (1982): 243-260.

3. B. Kilbourn and D.A. Roberts, *Science, Society and the Non-Academic Student: Phase I, Final Report.* (Ottawa: Social Science and Humanities Research Council, 1983). This work involved the observation of seven different, intermediate, general-level science classes. Each class was observed for the duration of a unit of material taught (an average of fifteen lessons per class) and all lessons were tape recorded and supplemented by field notes and interviews with teachers.

A Point of View on Feedback

Feedback is a complicated art comprising two major components. On the one hand, it is a phenomenon of human interaction. Issues of quality, interpretation, value, ethics, caring, intensity, genuineness, integrity, and power are present in the *process* of feedback just as they are, to varying degrees, in any interaction between people. On the other hand, feedback also has *substance*. It is always about something. The substance of feedback betrays values about what is worth giving feedback on.

No one goes into a feedback situation without an explicit or implicit perspective on what the interaction should be like and what issues might merit attention. Nor can anyone write a case study about feedback completely unaffected by her or his views about the process and substance. In this section I want to be as explicit as possible about my point of view on feedback as it guides my commentary about Oliver and Taylor's work together, my construction of the entire case, and, to some degree, Oliver and Taylor's interaction. The shape of Oliver and Taylor's interaction was, of course, heavily influenced by their own values and biographies, but it was also influenced by their understanding of the outcomes of the project described in the "Background" above. The findings of that project gave rise to some common assumptions regarding what the feedback process should involve, and what its substance should be. Although the expectations are by no means static — they were and are in a state of constant development and rethinking — their central features can be articulated and can help the reader understand why Oliver and Taylor say some of the things they do and why I make the comments I do.

Process

One expectation is that the tone of the feedback process will be descriptive and analytical rather than evaluative or judgmental, and that the teacher and participant-observer will work collaboratively on issues they have come to regard as significant in the given situation. Both participants need to pay attention to the context of the events of teaching and of the events of the feedback process itself. Both categories of events are to be the subject of inquiry when questions about what works and why are addressed. The long-term, concrete goal is for the teacher to be able to expect constructive feedback on significant issues when he or she wants it; the long-term attitudinal goal is that feedback comes to be seen not as an add-on or a burden, but as a useful and integral part of professional development over an entire career.

The several technical issues about feedback that arise in this case study and my ability to comment on them is partly due to my having the opportunity to look closely at the data and come to an understanding of the relationships among the events that were important to Oliver and Taylor. The luxury of having time to reflect allowed me to develop plausible hypotheses about what might have been the appropriate action in the context of a particular situation.

This case study has its spiritual roots in the early work on clinical supervision (although I have never liked that term) which was strongly influenced by counselling theory. On points about interactional technique in the feedback process I still find aspects of Robert Goldhammer's first edition of *Clinical Supervision* helpful.[1] Perhaps most important is the attitude of inquiry that Goldhammer brings to teaching and to feedback on teaching — it remains one of the more detailed accounts of feedback as a reflective process.

Substance

With regard to the substance of feedback, in this case study I wish to focus in particular on views about teaching students who do not relate well to academic learning — views that developed from our project team's earlier observations of intermediate general-level science classes.[2] The team's observations led us to think that teachers and students might benefit from constructive feedback on how the teaching, materials, and students interacted. Our observations suggested that it was not easy for teachers to maintain the coherence of the science units, in spite of that being one of the primary aims. The project team talked about coherence in terms of the students' ability to understand the material, and identified the need for *context* and *continuity*.

Context primarily refers to the background knowledge that a student needs in order to understand a point. Thus the idea of "context" is primarily an intellectual one. But there are a variety of contexts that a student must be aware of in order to make sense of classroom life. Substantive or intellectual, managerial, pedagogical, and interpersonal contexts seem, from our observations, to present difficulties for some students. Consequently, in those cases where students appeared not to understand what was happening, we asked what important context they might be missing. Although there is much "missing context" in academic settings that cannot be provided by the teacher, we were particularly interested in those situations where the teacher could help students understand their work by providing relevant context.

Continuity is closely related to context and concerns the minute-to-minute and lesson-to-lesson connections among the central ideas that students are expected to understand. (Again, the weight of meaning falls on the intellectual side, but continuity can also refer to other important dimensions of classroom life.) The theme of each unit provides a foundation for intellectual continuity; however, the brunt of the task of maintaining continuity falls on the teacher. We particularly noted those situations where a teacher's reminder of what had preceded and what was to follow helped students understand the material with which they were involved.

To be sure, there are all kinds of reasons why some students become disruptive or passive — it would be unreasonable to expect that materials and teaching which provided context and continuity could somehow magically turn non-productive learning situations on their head. And yet it is not unreasonable to think that uninteresting and disjointed materials and/or teaching might contribute to students' difficulty in learning and their lack of enthusiasm for the intellectual aspect of school.

Observations of the implementation of the units contributed to lively discussions between teachers and among the project team. We began to think of various teaching situations in terms of the role of *reasons* in teaching, especially how reasons affect the student's ability to understand that which is to be learned. It seemed that the job of providing context and continuity frequently involved giving reasons for things. Our thinking was influenced by people like Israel Scheffler[3] who argues that *giving reasons* is inherent to the concept of teaching. Although he speaks of reasons primarily in relation to intellectual substance, reasons can be seen more broadly as providing minute-to-minute, event-to-event, day-to-day continuity, in spite of shifts in the context within which things are said and done. Giving reasons can be seen as a central element maintaining continuity of meaning.[4]

The project team looked closely at reasons, context, continuity, and the communication of meaning in response to the observation of disengaged and disruptive students and empathy with their teachers. Because of constant temporal hiatuses and contextual shifts, we realized that a teacher may have to put considerable energy into maintaining an appropriate degree of continuity for students who, for whatever reasons, tend to engage (or tolerate) their school experiences as discrete episodic events. Maintaining intellectual continuity and providing the appropriate context *so that students can understand* is, in part, a matter of knowing both when and what kinds of reasons to give or solicit. Observations of general-level classes suggested that a teacher might need to utilize the types of reasons (broadly interpreted) outlined below.

Intellectual reasons

Intellectual reasons facilitate the student's comprehension of the subject matter. They clarify why such and such is the case, how one gets from A to B in a line of thinking, where a memorized fact fits in a general pattern, and what connects discrete bits of information. Reasons also counter some of the factors in the classroom which contribute to intellectual discontinuity, among the more common of which is the failure to connect intellectual threads which tie a series of lessons together. Interruptions like class pictures, eye tests, holidays, and PA announcements further compromise efforts to establish intellectual continuity.

Some discontinuities are inherently intellectual, as when a critical step in a line of reasoning is missing, or evidence is lacking, or connections are not made. Other discontinuities are more subtle and relate to a lack of context. For example:

> Students in a lab were having trouble seeing what was expected. Typical comments were, "What are we supposed to see?" and, "What are we looking for?" The teacher's response was, "Observe more carefully."
>
> However, circumstances indicated that the students were not inattentive, but did not know the context within which they were working. Their ability to understand *what* they were doing and *why* was inhibited by the teacher's reluctance to provide the context they needed.[5]

Such episodes may be particularly important for students who do not have a rich intellectual context to bring to bear on confusing situations like these, and who do not manufacture "missing context" (as students in advanced-level courses have been observed to do). In the present case study, intellectual reasons are regularly discussed by Oliver and Taylor in terms of providing context and continuity. For example, early on Oliver remarks to Taylor: "I thought you did a nice job of doing a lot of linkage with the lesson before, and also with what was to come. You were providing an awful lot of context" (dialogue line no. 19).

Pedagogical reasons

For any given instance of teaching a teacher has a particular approch or style or technique. Although teachers seldom talk in the classroom explicitly about their approach, they do have reasons for the pedagogical approach that they take. Pedagogical reasons explain why teaching is done as it is — why, for example, a sequence of activities is followed at a given time in a particular way. The "reasons" concern pedagogical circumstances rather than the nature of the subject matter. For instance, a teacher might say, "Normally we should proceed with the next three steps, but I want you to stop now; we have to clean up because we don't have time to complete the next stage and the materials will dry out if we leave them until tomorrow." In this instance, "normal procedure" is defined by the subject matter, and the *reason* for abandoning normal procedure is the pedagogical situation.

Shifts in context (from intellectual to pedagogical to managerial, etc.) are commonplace in the classroom, but they can inhibit continuity if students are not made aware of how the shifts relate to the intellectual point of a lesson. For instance, the intellectual point can be compromised when pedagogical reasons for doing things are not clear or become confused with intellectual substance:

> Students had to use the results of a distillation experiment as an integral part of an argument they were developing concerning water purification. The teacher did not have time to set up the equipment before the exercise and had the students assemble the apparatus themselves at the beginning of the forty-five minute period.

The teacher's reason for this approach was to save time. It was a *pedagogical* reason and not substantively related to the central intellectual point of the lesson. (One could, however, imagine the central point to be "learning how to set up the equipment," rather than to collect data and develop an argument, as was the case here.) But, having to set up the equipment and get it to work meant that a number of students did not have enough time to produce the relevant data. In addition, rather than helping set up the unfamiliar equipment, the teacher confused the intellectual and pedagogical contexts of the lesson by grilling students on the proper method of setting up the equipment. Their attention was diverted away from the intellectual intent of the lesson, and most students lost sight of why they were doing the exercise in the first place. Talk about pedagogical approaches is not common in classrooms, but there are occasions when pedagogical reasons, if made explicit by a teacher, can help students make sense of their classroom experience.

Oliver and Taylor do not use the term "pedagogical reason," but frequently their talk carries that meaning. For example, after telling the students that they have two cells to look at under the microscope, Taylor says to them, "I guess the real reason for having two is because I worry that if the lesson doesn't go very well . . . one is a backup for the other. But I have a couple of reasons for doing this today" (71). On another occasion Taylor "thinks out loud" to the students about the pedagogical choices he has to make:

> I will fiddle with these things tomorrow morning; if I can find something that represents cilia, I will keep it on the slide for period two. If I can't, I think we have to move on. It seems to me that also you just need more time at the microscopes. But the other thing that is pulling at me, of course, is [while] some

of you need more time at the microscopes to find them, there are the same number of people who are bored and they are ready to start horsing around again. [90]

Pedagogical and intellectual issues are frequently interwoven. In the following instance Taylor relates what the students are doing in their activities (a pedagogical issue) to the intellectual substance of the lesson — it can be seen that he is giving students reasons for what they are doing:

> [Drawing accurately] has nothing to do with whether or not you are a good artist, but the idea of whether the cell is like this, or whether it is like this with respect to its neighbour. . . . You see, the differences between a normal cell and a cancerous cell that we will be looking at later on may be such that if you are not careful about the way you draw the cells, by looking at the diagrams, the normal cell and the cancerous cell, you are not going to be able to see any difference. [111]

Managerial reasons

Teachers' actions in a classroom are often designed to maintain control and to keep a group of people working smoothly as a social unit. Classroom management routines establish a consistent method of interaction which resonates with most students' sense of fairness, proportion, and consistency, and which can be explained by managerial reasons. When management becomes overly punitive or when reasons for management routines are not apparent or convincing, the intellectual component of teaching can be sabotaged. More subtle are episodes where intellectual and management issues are confused. Geddis provides a good example when he shows how a student's train of thought was initially welcomed by a teacher, but eventually threatened the teacher's control.[6] The teacher closed the discussion by providing his "correct" answer, even though the student's contribution was equally acceptable. Such episodes can provoke intellectual discontinuity because the (unspoken) reasons for the teacher's interruption are managerial, although in the guise of substantive discussion.

Management is a fairly common topic of reflection and conversation for Oliver and Taylor, even though neither uses the term "managerial reasons." Here is an example of Taylor giving reasons for some managerial tasks: "I would like one person in the group to put the slides back and put them in the slide box and the other person to put the microscope away. Power off. Turn them onto low power. Mr. Brown is very concerned about them being under low power when you have finished" (242).

Interpersonal reasons

Interpersonal reasons "lie behind" a teacher's actions, and affect students' ability to acquire coherent meaning from their classroom experience. The students' sense of coherence is qreatly affected by a teacher's *sincerity* and *engagement* in an interaction. For example, a group of students who fell behind in their lab work were told by their teacher to make up the work after school, even though the necessary and complex equipment was disassembled and put away in cupboards, producing a situation where make-up would be difficult, time consuming, frustrating and, in the end, unlikely. The circumstances were such that the sincerity of the teacher's directive was questionable.

In another instance a student accidentally broke a breaker and started to clean it up. The teacher arrived and quizzed the student on correct clean-up procedure. The student looked puzzled. In this vignette the teacher responded with apparent concern for the student's safety, but the on-the-spot quiz and the intensity of the teacher's demeanor betrayed anger, not concern. In these kinds of episodes, the double message makes it difficult for the student to comprehend the interpersonal reality of the situation. Double messages are problematic from the standpoint of honest interaction, of course, but they can also contribute to intellectual discontinuity by interrupting intellectual flow and by leaving a student feeling uncertain about her or his understanding of the teacher's intent.

Interpersonal classroom relations are also determined by the degree to which a teacher is willing to engage students intellectually and emotionally. For example, in one class students who had been labelled "general" and were put together at a separate table were ignored unless they became disruptive. This was in spite of the fact that much of the time these students did not understand the material they were to learn, and were confused as to what they were to be doing. The teacher would literally keep a physical distance from these students or would be reluctant to talk with them (e.g., perfunctory conversation) — behaviour which is referred to as "Distancing."

The issues of sincerity and engagement are represented by Figure 1.

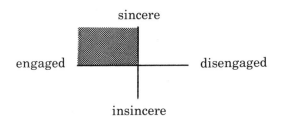

sincere

engaged   disengaged

insincere

Figure 1

Within this framework the teacher's task, interpersonally, is to try to keep communication within the upper-left quadrant. Insincerity and disengagement only occassionally appear to be issues for Oliver and for Taylor and his students. At one point in the process they discuss those students with whom Taylor seldom interacts during class discussion. This can be seen as an issue of "interpersonal engagement" although they do not specifically use that term. Nevertheless, Oliver and Taylor do talk about the interpersonal dynamics of the classroom, as seen in Taylor's comments about Steve: "Most of their interaction is . . . negative in what they're actually saying: put-down, put-down, put-down. And with Steve . . . I can't tell whether he's supporting *me*, or putting *them* down" (30). Taylor also talks more generally about his relationships with his students, making it clear that the interpersonal aspect of teaching is very important to him.

The kinds of reasons and the particular shape they have been given in the above discussion are a result of what was seen as problematic for many students in general-level courses. Teacher and student talk about reasons can be thought of as a response to the questions: "Why should I believe this?" or "Why should I do this?" Such questions are usually tacit. When overtly expressed, they are frequently not in a form or tone which might provoke a teacher's thoughtful consideration. And yet, even when hostilely or glibly put, such questions have a sincere core — they alert us to the likelihood that the student does not understand classroom experience in an intended way. These "why" questions are probably always present, whether overtly expressed or not and, at some level, they demand to be taken seriously. "Giving reasons" is one way of dealing with "why" questions and can be seen as taking the following forms:

Intellectual:

(Knowledge)   "The reason X is considered true is because. . . ."

(Skill)   "The reason you keep your eye on the ball is because. . . ."

Pedagogical: "The reason you must wash the test tubes again is because. . . ."

Managerial: "The reason I want only one person from each group at the table is because. . . ."

Interpersonal: "The reason I interrupted your story was. . . ."

These reasons are stylized to highlight that, from the student's standpoint, the unspoken reasons for what is happening in the classroom may not always be clear or credible. Being told what to do or think without reasons can be an affront to an individual and may be a particularly critical issue for adolescents who are trying to assimilate to adult life. "Giving reasons" is frequently lost sight of as an issue in the classroom which must be juxtaposed with the student's persistent, tacit questions *"Does this make sense?"* and *"Why am I doing this?"*

The complexity of issues around giving reasons renders this juxtaposition less than straightforward. For instance, even a teacher's best efforts to deal clearly with "why" questions may not be met with enthusiasm or be comprehended by some students. In addition, espoused reasons are not necessarily the "real" reasons for things; the "real" reasons may be complex and multiple. The distinction between "espoused" and "real" is at the heart of the issue of sincerity in the classroom. But, although the distinction is important and easily made, in actual instances it is frequently problematic. For example, looking at education in a broader sense, some would argue that much of what is done in school in the name of liberation is, in fact, not liberating at all but, rather, prepares students for mindless tasks in the work force.[7] In the Oliver and Taylor case study, "reasons" is usually used in a more restricted sense to refer to the intellectual connections among various aspects of the subject-matter and learning experiences, but the broader issues about reasons (e.g., whose, for what end, and with what assumptions about the nature and function of reasons) cannot be dismissed. Discourse about the power and role of reasons helps stimulate reflection about what it means to be a teacher, in general and at any given moment.

In a more methodological vein, to focus on the use of reasons in the classroom is not meant to imply that the teacher is always the one providing reasons. In some instances that may be appropriate, in others it may be that the teacher's role is to help students work out reasons. I would argue that it is the teacher's responsibility to be critically aware of issues in teaching that relate to the use of reasons, but by no means does this suggest that the teacher should be a giver of reasons and the student a passive receptor. It is frequently pointed out that too often students are not given a chance to explain and work out *their* reasons. Many contend that interactive teaching provides an atmosphere where that can happen. To some extent these issues are matters of style and approach and lie outside my main point about the general place and importance of *reasons as central to student understanding*. If taken seriously, such a stance requires that the teacher (at some point in the teaching/learning act) actively monitor for student understanding — the teacher must be sensitive to situations where issues of context, continuity, and reasons are problematic for students, and this is probably easier to do in interactive teaching.[8]

The focus on reasons is not intended to rule out spontaneity, intuitive judgement, and frivolous acts as normal and essential aspects of classroom life. It is meant to call our attention to the fact that if classroom life is to be comprehensible to students, and if they are to understand that which they are expected to learn, then the events of the classroom must be fundamentally reasonable.

For some teachers the idea of explicitly providing for intellectual coherence by addressing reasons where appropriate is integral to their instruction. For others it is not. And when students express frustration, some responses (e.g., punitive control) exacerbate the problem by directing attention away from intellectual substance.

It is important to remember, however, that many classroom situations are equally frustrating and difficult for the teacher. Even having to control a few potentially disruptive students in a class makes it difficult to respond to the intellectual needs of other students. This is nicely illustrated in the following two vignettes involving the same teacher in each case (not Taylor):

> In an advanced-level science class thirty students were working independently, typical of the teacher's style. Students were on task — there was a productive hum common to this class. The teacher occasionally circulated around the room and appeared unconcerned about students talking with one another and occasionally leaving their desks. It was a relaxed atmosphere. A student raised her hand, asked a question, and she and the teacher began a discussion. The teacher hunched over the front of her table with his back to three quarters of the class. He seemed to be involved in a complex explanation. The intensity of the conversation suggested that it was unlikely that he was aware of much else in the classroom for four to five minutes. The class proceeded as usual.

> At another time during the same day a general-level class of about twenty-five students was dealing with the same material with the same teacher. Students worked independently as in the previous class. This class was considerably quieter, however. The teacher "cruised" more often. Students did not leave their seats unless they asked permission. The teacher talked with the observer less frequently in this class and for shorter periods. When he did, he kept his eye on the class. He did not keep his back to the class. As with the other class, this class was impressive in how smoothly it seemed to run. But, there was one striking difference. When a student asked a question, the teacher did not engage her or him with a lengthy or a substantive reply. Questions tended to be dealt

with perfunctorily by directing students to their class notes or to the text, or with a suggestion to "think about it."

The focus on classroom management in the second episode required that the teacher intellectually distance himself from the students. Management situations that are potentially volatile are sometimes so intense that a teacher cannot monitor the whole situation and, at the same time, engage in discussion with a student. These students were, without a doubt, well "behaved" and exhibited few disruptive behaviours, but my observations of their work and conversation suggested that they had little understanding of what they were doing or why, in spite of the teacher's efforts to accommodate these needs. His lessons were designed for closure within one class period, and were activity oriented, which is inherently motivating. However, closure with every lesson runs the risk of episodic learning; the students may not see the connection between successive classes. And activity oriented lessons, by their very nature, produce conditions which require considerable management, leaving open the risk of emphasizing control and efficiency at the expense of understanding.

There are no simple solutions to these complex teaching situations, but the likelihood of episodic learning and compromised understanding can at least be minimized if a teacher can make explicit the kinds of connections that help students understand the different contexts within which events lie, and can provide reasons (intellectual, pedagogical, managerial, interpersonal) which give lessons and a unit continuity and coherence. The extent to which reasons can be provided depends upon what might be warranted given the particulars of a specific situation. It is the individual teacher who is in the best position to understand these particulars and act on them.

The complexities and demands of teaching suggest that if teachers are to address intellectual continuity with students, they need to support each other in using relevant sensitizing concepts to help them "see" what the daily demands of the classroom may prevent them from seeing. However, providing supportive and meaningful feedback is not easy to learn or to do. It is an art which is itself a good example of practice that can be informed by reflection and discussion. A detailed documentation of an instance of the constructive feedback process is likely to be a useful point of reference for teachers who want to work together on teaching.

---

1. Robert Goldhammer, *Clinical supervision*, 1st ed. (New York: Holt, Rinehart, & Winston, 1969). For a more recent update on the status of clinical supervision see: W. J. Smyth, ed., *Learning About Teaching Through Clinical Supervision* (London: Croom Helm Ltd., 1986).

2. See note 3, p. 4. Observations and discussions in *Phase I* included the following team: Ted Anderson, Bruce Curtis, Art Geddis, Brent Kilbourn, Allan MacKinnon, Tom McCaul, and Doug Roberts.

3. I. Scheffler, "The Concept of Teaching," in *Concepts of Teaching: Philosophical Essays*, ed. C. J. B. Macmillan and T. W. Nelson (Chicago: Rand-McNally & Co., 1968), pp. 17-27. "To teach, in the standard sense, is at some points at least to submit oneself to the understanding and independent judgment of the pupil, to his [or her] demand for reasons, to his sense of what constitutes an adequate explanation. To teach someone that such and such is the case is not merely to try to get him to believe it: deception, for example, is not a method or a mode of teaching. Teaching involves further that, if we try to get the student to believe that such and such is the case, we try also to get him to believe it for reasons that within the limits of his capacity to grasp, are *our* reasons. Teaching, in this way, requires us to reveal our reasons to the student and, by so doing, to submit them to his evaluation and criticism" (p. 17).

4. T. Russell draws on the work of S. Toulmin and R. S. Peters to argue for the place of reasons in the classroom. See: T. Russell, "Analyzing Arguments in Science Classroom Discourse: Can

Teachers' Questions Distort Scientific Authority?" *Journal of Research in Science Teaching* 20(1), (1983): 27- 45.

5. All of the examples in this section are taken from field notes of classroom observations. Examples from the Oliver and Taylor case will be specifically identified.

6. A. Geddis, *Perspectives on Knowledge in the Classroom: A Case Study in Science Teaching* (Ed.D. diss., University of Toronto, 1985).

7. See, for example, Roger Simon, "What Schools Can Do: Designing Programs for Work Education That Challenge the Wisdom of Experience," *Journal of Education* 169(3), (1987): 101–116.

8. I am implicitly contrasting interactive teaching with what is sometimes called lecture or teacher monologue or transmission teaching. One reason that constant teacher monologue is frequently disparaged as a mode of teaching is that it leaves little room for monitoring student understanding. An interactive mode is no guarantee that student understanding will be the focus of attention, of course; it depends upon substance and manner. Douglas Barnes is particularly illuminating on these issues in his discussion of the contrast between transmission and interpretation. See his *From Communication to Curriculum* (Harmondsworth: Penguin Books Ltd., 1976).

Foreground

A t the time of this case study, Taylor had been teaching general science and biology in various schools within the local school system for nine years. He was in his early thirties, had been trained as a biology teacher, and was respected for being able to relate interpersonally to students in general-level courses. During regular class periods Taylor tended to do most of the talking, interrupting his instruction to briefly answer questions. During labs he would circulate around the classroom and work with students individually. He had an informal personal style, was receptive to students' questions, and interacted with them freely outside the classroom. Taylor had been observed and given feedback on several occasions during his career. He was involved in the early stages of this project (which resulted in the "point of view" outlined above) and volunteered to work with Oliver.

Oliver, in his late thirties, was a highly respected department head and biology teacher who had experience with the feedback process as outlined in the preceding sections. In this case he was a participant-observer with the level of participation varying from day to day. When there were lab activities his classroom participation was considerable. When Taylor's teaching was didactic or involved some form of discussion with students, Oliver's role was more strictly observational. As will become apparent, outside the class period itself Oliver played a supportive role.

Although Oliver did not take part in earlier phases of the project, he had followed the process closely and was interested, from the standpoint of staff development, in getting involved. He could be described as a fairly intense person, kindly, energetic, and extremely conscientious. Oliver and Taylor had not always been at the same school, but had been colleagues at other schools. Oliver had been temporarily seconded to the school board's central administration which gave him the necessary time to participate with Taylor.

On several occasions I discussed with both men the nature of the work in which they were to become central figures. Two weeks before beginning the project, the three of us met for a day to talk about the background and our point of view on the whole project, and to outline a tentative teaching plan for the first few days of the unit Taylor had selected. (Both had been given the project proposal as well as the results of earlier observational work, including the synopses of teaching science in general-level courses from which the above point of view emerged.) It was understood that Oliver would provide feedback on such issues as the context and continuity of the unit on cancer and cell biology. Taylor would try to articulate the reasons behind his chosen classroom style and would elaborate upon relevant aspects of the context surrounding his teaching. No preferred model of teaching was assumed during Oliver and Taylor's work together. The process was to be conducted within the parameters of Taylor's own plans and style.

Each class was observed by Oliver, who also made notes, and all classes but one were taped. (None of the classes was observed by me, although I had seen Taylor teach on previous occasions.) After each class Oliver and Taylor talked about what had happened and made plans for the next lesson. These conferences usually lasted an hour and also were taped. Selected quotes from the tapes of the lessons and conferences constitute the bulk of the descriptive aspect of this account. In addition, I taped three interviews with Taylor and four with Oliver. These interviews gave me a sense of what was significant to each participant as he engaged the process and, ultimately, they served as the basis for selecting and analysing data and for structuring the presentation of the case study.

This case study focusses on the feedback process between Oliver and Taylor, and understanding the interaction between Taylor and his students in the classroom provides a context for interpreting Oliver's and Taylor's interactions. It is important to remember that the following day-by-day descriptions of the lessons are sketches. Much information that would be pertinent if *teaching*, rather than feedback, was the central issue in the account has been omitted. This work is not an attempt to characterize teachers in general, nor Oliver and Taylor in particular, nor students in general-level courses. (The class was a grade ten general-level science course. There were nineteen students officially enrolled, although there were usually about fifteen present on any given day.) The information included in the sketches of the lessons has been selected (a) to illustrate issues of continuity, and (b) to provide a context for Taylor and Oliver's conversations.

There are several themes that run through the case study which are critical to an understanding of the feedback process:

• As a backdrop to the study, it is necessary to take into account what it means to have a disruptive student in class, and what it is like to work with students who are not enthusiastic about school.

• The primary focus of this case study in NOT Taylor's teaching; it is important to remember that the raison d'être of any feedback process concerns the interests of the students who have little control over their schooling. The substantive issues of coherence, reasons, context, continuity, and meaning are discussed in recognition of students' interests.

• Considering context, continuity, reasons, coherence, and meaning is vital if teaching is to be comprehensible to students; how these elements of teaching are considered is reflected in the manner in which teaching is conducted. Although in this case the terms themselves are not Oliver and Taylor's, the emphasis on making teaching comprehensible to students is a principle to which they would both readily subscribe. But it is one thing to subscribe to a principle in the abstract and another thing to come to terms with what that principle means in particular situations. Oliver and Taylor can agree about the importance of continuity while they might agree less readily about what constitutes an instance of continuity. All of this is made more complicated by the fact that these are not absolute concepts. They are relative to time, place, individual students, and a myriad of other factors — they are relative to the real situations with which Oliver and Taylor must deal.

• The significant meaning of abstractions such as context and continuity comes from their interplay with practice. Blumer distinguishes between absolute and relative concepts using the terms "definitive" and "sensitizing" — sensitizing concepts are those that give "the user a general sense of reference and guidelines in approaching empirical instances. Where definitive concepts provide prescriptions of what to see, sensitizing concepts merely suggest directions along which to look."[1] Terms like "context," "continuity," "reasons," and "coherence" are sensitizing concepts which provide direction for Taylor in his teaching and for Oliver in his feedback. They give form to the particulars of the situation with which Oliver and Taylor are involved. In turn, the actual instances in the live situation provide empirical grounding for what the terms mean for that situation. There is a constant and natural interplay between the abstract terms used to talk about practice and the particulars of that practice — theory informs practice while practice informs theory.

• Thus, as Oliver and Taylor work through the feedback process, they grapple with the question of what things must be said and done with the students in order to provide for context and continuity (in the interest of helping the students understand) while, at the same time, they struggle with the question of what counts as an instance of, say, continuity.

• This account should not be read without reflecting on the daily stresses faced by a teacher: constant interruptions to the momentum of a lesson and to daily routine, the incredible pace of daily life, and the many obligations outside the classroom which are integral to the smooth functioning of a school all contribute to stress.

• The personal life of Taylor is not the focus of this case study, but what we do as teachers is interwoven with who we are as persons and with our life outside our paid work. The complex relationship between the professional and the personal is essential to understand if we are to become artful with feedback.

• Much that has been written about feedback (peer coaching, etc.) tends to emphasize the delicate interactional aspects of the process. But equally important is the substance of feedback and the role that the subject matter plays in any feedback conference. Considered implicitly in this entire case study is the significance of the integrity of the subject matter and its relationship to the feedback process.

• An overall theme running through this account concerns the *integration* of the various threads that form the fabric of teaching. The nature of the students, the social context of schools and classrooms, the teacher's personal context, the nature of the subject-matter, the teacher's professional "know-how," and how the teacher works with concepts and ideas about the subject-matter and about teaching are all part and parcel of what a teacher is and what a teacher does. At any given moment one aspect may assume prominence over others, but almost never do these concerns fade from the teacher's tacit awareness. Part of the reason that the account is as detailed as it is and includes so much conversation by Oliver and Taylor is to let the interrelatedness of these elements show through. If we are to work seriously on understanding teaching and feedback on teaching that sense of interrelatedness cannot be neglected.

• Fundamental to this case study is a recognition of the complexity of the feedback process and the sense in which it is a real *art* — an art which continues to be learned over a professional lifetime of practice. The complexities of the process are important to document because, without actual instances to consider, they can easily be overlooked. As will be seen, the process requires skill and technique, vision and wisdom, and attention to the dialectical relationship between abstract concepts used to think about practice and practice itself. In addition, although the process is intended to be collegial, there is always the question of differential power in a relationship; the present and past history of the relationship between a teacher and an observer is integral to what happens at any given point in the process. *Such complexities are a normal part of the multi-facetted feedback process.* Following the ups and downs of Oliver and Taylor's work together provokes serious questions which can guide a reader through the varied terrain of this case and of the feedback process generally:

* What issues should be discussed?

* How much should be talked about during a conference?

* How hard should an observer push on an issue, if at all?

* How explicit should issues be made?

* What are the boundaries of discussion?

* How should the observer view the teacher's world?

* How involved should the observer be in the teacher's personal life?

* What should be the criterion of success with regard to the process?

There are no general answers to these questions, but they will likely have to be considered by participants as they work with the process. An assumption of this case study is that detailed instances of practice provide a basis for reflection and can contribute to an understanding and improvement of future practice.

---

1. H. Blumer, "What is Wrong With Social Theory?" *American Sociological Review* 19 (1954): 7. Quoted in M. Hammersley and P. Atkinson, *Ethnography: Principles in Practice* (London: Tavistock, 1983), p. 180.

Thursday, Day 1

Beginning the Process

In the following day-by-day account of teaching a unit on cancer and cell biology particularly significant issues will be noted in these boxes. For example, notice Taylor's concern with being "on-topic," and the tension between wanting student participation but not wanting erroneous information brought into the discussion. Also, note how student disruptions impede intellectual continuity. Oliver's central role is to listen carefully during the conference.

Class

The study of the cell, required in most biology programs, can be a dull topic for many students. With this in mind, a unit was developed for general-level courses using the topic of cancer to enliven the study of cell biology, and showing the relevance of cell biology to understanding the diagnosis, cause, and treatment of cancer. The unit was developed by science teachers wanting to maintain intellectual continuity and motivational interest in general-level courses. Designed as a teacher's guide, it consisted of a sequence of topics accompanied by suggestions for activities, worksheets, films, filmstrips, labs, readings, and teaching strategies. No formal homework or test items were included. The unit had been used by a few teachers for several years, and although each had adapted it to her or his own use, there had been no revisions made to the trial edition.

While the information and activities in the unit followed a logical sequence, a teacher would have to invest considerable effort to maintain the intellectual continuity of the unit. For example, the unit started with a general discussion of cancer; next were activities on learning how to use a microscope so that students could examine normal cells; normal cells were examined in order to learn about cell structure and function, which, in turn, were to be discussied in order to begin learning about abnormal (cancerous) cells. Mindlessly following this sequence could mean that after the first discussion about cancer five or more days would pass before students heard about that topic again.

The structure of the unit, in its draft form, ran the risk of any day's lesson being regarded by a student as an episodic bit, unconnected to previous and future work. In order to maintain intellectual continuity a teacher would have to work hard at making connections, asking appropriate questions, and providing reasons, (e.g., "Remember, as we discussed yesterday, one reason that we study the structure and function of normal cells is . . . ") so that students would see each day's activities as part of a coherent whole. In short, the unit was not one that a teacher could use without considerable thought and work. This was the first time Taylor had taught this cancer/cell biology unit, although he had taught cell biology every year of his career.

Taylor started the class by introducing the unit on cancer and cells and by expressing his concern that discussion not get off-topic (e.g., "If I am in the middle of talking about a cell and you want to know about lung cancer, maybe we can talk together after class, so we don't get too off-topic)."[1] Because Taylor had found in the past that students frequently had misconceptions about cancer, his strategy was to focus initial discussion around the following five questions: "What is cancer? Is cancer contagious? Can you inherit cancer? What are some typical symptoms? Is cancer curable?" Before the first question he polled the class:

1   **T**   *Just out of interest, a show of hands, can anybody tell me if there has been an incidence of cancer in their immediate family: grandparents, uncles, aunts? Has there been cancer in your family?* [show of hands] *That is an interesting number. Jim, I really don't want the competition, OK. Now, we could talk about personal experiences, I think probably a little bit later on; I have a case study that I want you to look at.*

       Can somebody tell me what cancer is? Does anybody have an idea? Bob, Jim, I don't want you to have your own conversation again while I am teaching. We have gone over this before; if you guys want to argue, argue in the parking lot or the cafeteria, but not here. I am sorry.

After brief discussion of what cancer is, Taylor again indicated his desire to stay on track:

2   **T**   *Bob, again that is a good example. You are skipping ahead and treating a specific type of cancer, which is something that will take us off topic. So I am going to be really rotten and not answer your question. If you want to talk after class, that is fine. . . . Now, a lot of people have some misconceptions about cancer. One thing about it that I would like to ask you is, how many people here would say that cancer is contagious, that you can get it from somebody else? Well, that is good. . . . It is nice to see that all of you have got that sorted out. It is not contagious. Can you inherit cancer from your parents?*

At this point Taylor gave a fairly lengthy talk on the inheritability question. He referred to the role of the "oncogene" and pointed out that, while cancer is not inherited,

3   **T**   *. . . what you can inherit is a gene that will program a cell to be cancerous. . . . So, in other words, this is a bit of very detailed information I am throwing at you for why they have qualified "inherited" — they say you can inherit a tendency to get cancer. . . .*

The discussion moved to the questions of whether cancer is curable and what are typical symptoms (Taylor wrote appropriate responses on the board):

4   **S**   *How about vomiting, Sir?*

5   **T**   *What I was going to summarize here was chronic illness. Vomiting, OK. Sores that don't heal. Good, John. Lumps, somebody said. Let's stop the list there, simply because we have indicated some examples and we are starting to talk about some very specific types of cancer. . . . That's OK, they are good examples. That is good. I am impressed. I find you seem to know a lot more about it than some people have in the past. Now, cures? What do you know about how cancer can be cured?*

After a brief discussion and listing of cures for cancer, Taylor gave each student a mimeographed sheet on cancer (which he read) and a sheet of five questions to answer. The answer to the fifth question ("How are cancer cells different from normal cells?") was not found in the material they had just read, nor was it discussed in class.

6   **T**   *Let's just take this up real quick. Based on . . . the reading, you should have gotten the answers. The last question provides a slight problem.* [The students verbally answer the first four questions and then move to the fifth.] *OK, go ahead. How are cancerous cells different from normal body cells?*

7   **S₁**   *Cancer cells are different from body cells because a normal cell is red but cancer cells are white because they are dead.*

8   **T**   *Interesting.*

9   **S₂**   *But that was wrong.*

At that moment Taylor appeared reluctant to readily agree with the second student's comment that the response was wrong.

10   **T**   *You know, that poses a problem, and I am not picking on you here, but the point is that you have to rely on what you* know *for this question, don't you? You are writing down what you know, not necessarily what I would like to hear, but what you know. . . .*

Taylor faced a common dilemma in teaching: he was concerned that telling students they are wrong (especially when the "correct" response is not obviously available) would inhibit their active participation, but, at the same time, did not want the class to be trading erroneous information. After several interchanges Taylor suggested that the question was one which the class could better answer at the end of the unit rather than on the first day.

Taylor ended the lesson by making a distinction between benign and malignant tumors and defining the term "metastasis." During his talk, Bill and Steve started to act up.

11   **T**   *You can grab that tumor by the membrane and pull the whole thing out, OK? Those are the characteristics of a benign tumor. A malignant tumor, on the other hand, is not the same at all. Bill, Steve, come on back. Come on guys, please. I want to finish this today. I need your co-operation. Malig-*

nant tumors are different because there is no membrane and the cells that are cancerous grow into or invade the surrounding tissue rather than pushing it out of the way. So within a given space you have a mixture of cancerous and normal cells — they are mixed together. Of course that presents problems if you are doing surgery beause you have to cut an area of tissue out that is bigger than where the cancer is to make sure you have got it all. . . .

At the end of class Taylor asked for questions and one student asked if a developing fetus could get cancer from the mother. Taylor provided considerable context in terms of the relationship between the womb, placenta, and fetus, and the functions of the immune system. He ended by saying:

12   **T**   *I don't know the answer, whether or not a cancer can spread across the placenta and go into the blood stream like a metastasis, land in the baby, and the baby then not recognize the cancer, and it continues. I don't know. I have never heard of it, but I have never heard that it is impossible either. Anything else? Any other questions? Well, see you tomorrow.*

Conference

This account of Oliver and Taylor's conversation about the class is my reconstruction based on Oliver's field notes and my discussions with him. Oliver solicited and listened to Taylor's views of how the lesson went. He noted that all of the material Taylor had planned to cover had been covered and addressed Taylor's concern about getting off-topic, pointing out that, in his view, that had not happened. Taylor reiterated his concern that students often have misconceptions about cancer and noted that, "We did spend time on misleading information also — the red versus white cells idea." However, both he and Oliver acknowledged that, overall, the students seemed to have a good working knowledge of the subject.

Taylor was happy with how the lesson had gone. He indicated that the lesson was somewhat off the cuff and not flow-charted as was usual for him, hence there was some jumping around. He wondered about the fruitfulness of talking about the "on-cogene" so early in the unit. He noted that there was usually more teacher-student interaction and that he normally spent more time managing the group than he did during this lesson. He pointed out five students who were chronically difficult to handle. Oliver commented that Taylor seemed quite relaxed in spite of the interruptions and his presence. Taylor explained that the bantering back and forth was part of his style: "I do this more than some. Teacher X at [another school] won't even let the grade ten general students talk; if they do, they get a detention. I prefer a relaxed atmosphere which allows student expression."

The remaining minutes of the conference were used to plot the major events for the next several days. Taylor thought out loud about what he might do, indicating a desire to give the students access to hands-on material. The plan was to talk about a case history of cancer the next day (Friday) and introduce students to the care and use of the microscopes. He predicted that it was likely the students would be somewhat hyper on Friday because that evening was the Spring Festival, a much celebrated occasion at the school. On Monday and Tuesday he intended to have students look at prepared slides of cancer and then of live paramecium.

Considerations

Throughout this case study my focus is the feedback process between Oliver and Taylor. In addition to the documented interaction between them, a discussion about feedback is carried in these "Considerations" sections at the end of each day. Although the selection of data and construction of the entire account are clearly interpretive acts, the "Considerations" sections consciously move away from a descriptive orientation and introduce my own opinions, reflections, commentary, and asides on issues exemplified in the data. I note issues about the process that seem worthy of consideration, especially with regard to Oliver's influence on the unfolding events and to what emerged from my private interviews with each man.

The "Considerations," then, are a way of raising issues. They are not comments on the "rightness" of Oliver's and Taylor's actions in any given instance. My "advice" should be seen as an effort to parsimoniously present an issue for consideration and provide an instance of the issue I am raising. I take it for granted that there could be other interpretations of the events and that my reflections will simply assume a place among others as food for thought.

The first consideration I want to raise concerns the effect of "interruptions" on the intellectual continuity and coherent flow of a lesson. These interruptions are a constant factor in the fabric of classroom life; on this first day of the unit on cancer and cell biology Oliver noted *eight* outside interruptions to Taylor's lesson: the phone rang twice, on several occasions another teacher could be heard from the adjoining open-concept lab, Taylor had to leave briefly for coloured chalk, another teacher interrupted with a question. These were all brief interruptions and would likely be no more nor less than expected in any school. There was no obvious evidence that the interruptions were problematic; and yet it is hard to believe that such interruptions do not compromise the continuity and coherence of the students' intellectual experiences in the classroom.

---

1. Quotes are in sequence unless stated otherwise. In some cases quoted material has received minor editing to improve readability. Ellipses indicate a range of editorial deletions, but usually no more than four or five statements within the context of a particular topic of conversation.

Friday, Day 2

Feedback Overload

Oliver observes the strong links Taylor has established between case studies of cancer and the previous day's work, but questions the success of the microscope demonstration (which becomes more of an issue in subsequent lessons). Note the difference in Oliver's feedback style and the tendency toward "overload."

Class

C lass began with Taylor reading a case history of lung cancer during which he made connections to the class' work on the previous day and defined terms from the reading (e.g., "malignant," "pathologist," "autopsy"). He brought to class a model torso so students could examine the lungs and bronchial system, and he sketched diagrams on the board of the air-sac structure of the lung. Several students talked among themselves and were chastised by Steve (a student). Taylor discussed a case history of cancer within his own family, and a third case history he knew personally. During this time (approximately two thirds of the hour) Oliver noted a very high interest level.

The focus changed when Taylor moved to the topic of microscopes. He had intended to have each student study and label a diagram of a microscope in order to learn its parts. However, he ran short of time and did the exercise as a demonstration. He held up and talked about a microscope in front of the class while the students looked at a mimeographed diagram at their seats. Unfortunately, the students' microscope diagram did not correspond to the particular scope being demonstrated and most of their questions related to that disparity. Oliver noted that student interest flagged during this portion of the lesson. He observed that the connection between the case histories of cancer and the microscope was not made sufficiently explicit and was likely not clear to the students.

Conference

The conference began with a discussion of the gap in intellectual continuity for students who are absent from class, an issue over which a teacher has little control. The following comments are a forceful reminder of this aspect of working with some students:

13 **T**   *Did you notice, Jim, the student who walked in late? I told him he needed a book. He never came back.*

14 **O**   *No, I didn't notice that.*

15 **T**   *He never came back, so I'm going to have to go after him. At the beginning of the semester he was always attending. Mouthy. He and Steve. You noticed yesterday he and Steve going at it.*

16 **O**   *Yeah.*

17 **T**   *He's always been like that. Except all of a sudden he got suspended for something, fighting or something. They suspend for lateness now, so I'm not quite sure. There are more suspensions than we used to have. What I notice is happening is there are a whole rash of them. Allison is the same. She never missed a day until she got suspended and now she just won't come back to talk to the vice-principal. And I think Jim's attendance and behaviour have dropped right off since he got suspended. He's been missing about two days a week. He wasn't here Monday, he wasn't here Tuesday, he wasn't at the zoo, he was here yesterday with no note. He wasn't here Wednesday because he was at some athletic meet, so of course that covers all the other days. And he comes in late today and takes off. So I definitely have to start working through the office on that.*

Unfortunately you lose kids in the spring. You lose kids once the good weather comes and once the course has gotten to a certain point. And it's funny how it tails off.

18 **O**   *And it's hard to get them back.*

After this discussion, Oliver commented on the early portion of the lesson as it related to context and continuity:

19 **O**   *One thing I really found useful, initially, was you talking about the case study and reading that introduction to it, that one page. I thought you did a nice job of doing a lot of linkage with the lesson before, and also with what was to come. You were providing an awful lot of context. As you were going through those sheets you were defining words for kids. You were saying, "Yesterday, remember we talked about metastasis, we talked about this, that, and the other thing." And you defined a whole series of things which I think the kids really got into. Things like "pathologist," which you didn't mention yesterday; you took the time to define that. So you're providing context, you're also providing continuity with yesterday's lesson.*

Oliver introduced the possibility of using of a set of transparencies which Taylor had mentioned during the lesson, but had not used. Taylor's comment is interesting because it reveals an important aspect of the environment within which he works.

20 **T**   *This happens every time when you're teaching. You link into it and you*

remember from last year. You go through your file, it's labelled "cancer." I open the file, there's the sheet. I say "Ah, this is good! The stuff I've got in this file, this is good." I take it out and photocopy it and I take it into class. When I skimmed it . . . [I thought] — "The transparencies! — wouldn't it be nice if I [had them]." And I didn't go out and get it, primarily for reasons of classroom management. I figured if I go out to a physics building now, and unlock it, go in and look for them, you know, it's just too tight. You saw how I dashed to get the other stuff. I think you've got to keep it tight . . . for me as a teacher with Spring Festival, with the running around and the things on my mind, I haven't got the depth of preparation to the course, which might have involved having the transparencies out and an overhead. And having the torso, and having it all in there. That's the kind of thing that's missing because of all this stress of Spring Festival. But it's OK.

Oliver then complimented Taylor on the use of the torso and his effort to involve students:

21 **T** *Well, I initiated that by saying, "Steve, would you like to do me a favour and put [the torso] back together for me," and he said, "I don't know if I can." I said, "It's quite a challenge" and "Go ahead. Give it a try." So I initiated that. I'd want very much for them to feel that it's not a "hands off," you know, because it's the biology equipment. So, sometimes you give students things to do to keep busy. Sometimes you give them things to do to help you. This I tend to do to sort of say, "It's not off limits."*

At this point, Oliver commented that the diagram of the alveolus (air sac) Taylor had drawn on the board was not visible to most students. Taylor pointed out that the diagram was a quick sketch drawn to help him explain an aspect of the lung. It was not intended to make sense on its own, nor did he expect the students to copy it ("they didn't have their notebooks at that time, you may have noticed").They wouldn't be held accountable for it on a test. Oliver persisted:

22 **O** *To be honest, and to honour the student, you know, the kids at the back of the room couldn't see it. So, therefore, if you tacitly assume that you have provided them with some data, some evidence or something, and they can't see it, that is one of the gaps in context as I see it. And we all do it.*

After several interchanges in which Taylor restated this perception of what he was doing, Oliver reiterated what he perceived the whole process to be about:

23 **O** *This comes back to the whole issue of context and continuity, and I guess the reason that you and I are working on this is the fact that, you know, there will be gaps and we all do it. And it's nice for me to be able to bring it up and you can deal with it whatever way you want. You can just say, "Well, it's not that important at this point in time, I'm not going to deal with it at all. I may come back to it later on." Fair enough. All I'm trying to do — and I'm not trying to be critical, please don't take it that way — I'm just trying to raise issues and you deal with them whatever way you want.*

After complimenting Taylor on the use of an analogy, Oliver questioned why he did not pursue it. Taylor's reason was based on his intention to stay on track:

24   **T**   *I think what I was trying to do was just . . . make an instant application and. . . . I dropped it because I thought I'd done enough. . . . But, you know, [with that analogy I was potentially] getting really off topic and so I brought it right back.*

The conversation turned to a discussion of Steve's support of Taylor and why Taylor had made a critical comment to Steve. Taylor provided a broader context for understanding the incident and articulated the dilemma he faced in trying to interpret Steve's actions:

25   **O**   *Steve is a fascinating guy. As you're talking you may not hear him, but I did because I was closer.*

26   **T**   *I know that it's happening the whole time.*

27   **O**   *That's alright. But it's interesting the way he supports you. There was at least two or three instances where he would say, "Come on guys . . . smarten up."*

28   **T**   *He told them to smarten up, yeah.*

29   **O**   *Now here's the interesting thing. Steve says, "Why are we going in this direction," and you retorted, "You have very selective hearing."*

30   **T**   *I think that was because I said why we were going to do it and then he said, "Why are we going to do it," and I explained it again and he said, "Well, why are we going to do it." And so I guess I probably should have kept that comment to myself, but I thought, geez, he's got very selective hearing. And it was his agenda, there, to monopolize the conversation or to kind of . . . well, he's the master of the put-down. He's the master of the derogatory comment, you know. That's why.*

I appreciate his support. There's a little bit of getting on the bandwagon and criticizing there, because often they throw insults at each other from the back. Between him and Jim. It's one of those things that I see so often with kids that age. Most of their interaction is . . . negative in what they're actually saying: put-down, put-down, put-down. And with Steve . . . I can't tell whether he's supporting me, *or putting them* down.

31   **O**   *Maybe you should ask him.*

32   **T**   *Yeah, maybe I should. . . . It's not his answer so much as the fact that I suggest . . . [he] think about it. I think it's a good point. . . . And he learns. He does so much of the learning with his head down. Not asleep, not eyes closed, not head on the table. Arms on the table, head down, looking down*

> *at the floor. Alert and listening. . . . I've tried to change his behaviour, and I've backed off. I haven't given up, I've backed off, because I realize he's learning, he's listening. He's doing well. He reproduces this stuff. It appears magically in his notebook although he appears not to be working at it. But he wants the rest of the class to perceive him as, you know, head down. That's what I get out of it anyway. And because he does [listen], he's not a D student, he's an A student. He's getting an A. He's always got his homework done, he does good tests.*

Oliver commented that he sensed one of the students wanted to talk personally about cancer after Taylor had talked about his two case histories.

33   **O**   *I really got the feeling that John wanted to talk about cancer in his family. He talked about his grandfather on several occasions. He was obviously wanting to engage you and talk to you about it. And I think that if you had given him the opportunity he would have trotted out some of the feelings that he has about his own family. And that might have been nice to put [the subject of cancer] in the student context.*

34   **T**   *You know why I didn't? I was watching the clock and I was running behind.*

35   **O**   *Fair enough. OK.*

36   **T**   *And I had the agenda of switching to the microscope. . . .*

37   **O**   *It's easier with hindsight. . . .*

38   **T**   *As I say, and you know, there are so many limitations. Some classes you just wish they were over. Other classes you just don't have enough time. And what I felt was important to do was to be at a point where on Monday they could take the microscopes out and handle them and use them without a significant amount of time being taken explaining the microscope. So, I achieved my objectives of the amount I wanted to cover and, well, at the expense of John in this instance.*

It becomes clear in this interchange that, while an observer may have insights into what might have been done differently, it is the teacher who likely has the keenest temporal sense of the lesson. What Oliver did not say was that John's story could have been heard instead of Taylor's second story. But, as can be seen in the following discussion concerning the microscopes, once a teacher is committed to a particular lesson plan, it is not always easy or feasible to alter that plan. Taylor's quandary was whether to continue an interesting class discussion about cancer or move on to the microscopes:

39   **O**   *How do you feel they attended to what you were doing with the parts of the microscope?*

40   **T**   *It's not the best way to do it first of all. And again, I didn't have enough*

time. My agenda today was to get out all the microscopes, give out a prepared slide, show them how to get [the microscope] into focus, and go through all the parts and have [the diagram] labelled. What I did was I ran too long. You'll notice on the tape I said that at least twice. I took much longer than I thought I would because I really went into that case study I read. . . . I was just going to read through it, one run through, and spend fifteen minutes.

[The second] case study I thought was going to go really quickly, but we spent more time on it. And right there I thought, "OK, no way am I going to get everybody up and over to get the microscopes . . . because they're just going to be down and then [will have to go] back in." So I picked one microscope up and did it myself. Not as good, but again, I wanted to do it today. . . . I should have had them all out, everybody with their microscope at their table, because, you know, it should be hands-on, experiential. . . . But I was running out of time . . . I didn't feel I had enough filler to just not do the microscope at all today. Looking back, maybe at eleven minutes after eleven I should have thought, "Not enough time, let's go on talking about cancer." I wasn't sure whether . . .

41   **O**   *Well that's a judgement that you make and, you know, maybe you've trotted it out and you felt the kids at that point in time wouldn't take to this and you wanted to give them a different slate, fair enough. You know, sometimes it works and sometimes it doesn't.*

In the final minutes of the conference Taylor and Oliver commented on the difference between students in advanced and general-level courses as it related to the disparity between the diagram students had in front of them and to the microscope that Taylor used as a demonstration. Taylor noted this difference, but also noted the difference between a student and a teacher with experience, and the amount of time he had for preparation.

42   **O**   *They don't match and so a lot of the questions you got were because the diagram that you showed them was not the exact representation of the microscope.*

43   **T**   *I know.*

44   **O**   *And that's what the general level kids freak out on.*

45   **T**   *Well, it's a combination of the developmental difference between teacher and student, because, of course, as adults with a lot of previous experience, we're much more prepared to say, "That happens most of the time." You adjust very quickly, partly because you're older. And maybe it's also this advanced/general difference, an academic student, you know, they can handle it more. . . . But there's a teacher/student thing too. Because, of course, I whipped out [the diagram] and thought, "Great, no way am I going to sit down and draw a diagram if I've got this one". . . . Like, how come all [these diagrams aren't] perfectly tailored to us? I don't understand.*

46   **O**   *That's right. We do have a diagram in [another course] that's the same one as the microscope that you're running.*

47   **T**   *Well I was aware of that and, with the amount of time I had today, there just wasn't any time to dig for it.*

The closing comments are important in the context of Taylor's teaching style and later episodes in the case. Taylor and Oliver were talking about several of the troublemakers in the class.

48   **T**   *It sorts itself out one way or another. Either they sabotage, or they respect you, or they have to take science next semester because they've been thrown out of the class. I mean that's really what happens to a lot of these kids. You know John got thrown out of his geography [class] today because he was chatting to the guy next to him. Well, look at the difference between teaching styles. He'd be gone, he'd be out of the school if I decided to do the same thing. He'd be out of the school. Two teachers, that's enough. John belongs in school.*

Considerations

One issue in this conference is the shift in approach from that of Day 1. In the first conference, Oliver could be characterized as a receptive listener whose primary function was to clarify the nature of the events with the teacher and clarify the teacher's attitudes and feelings about those events. In Day 2 that stance shifts to one of taking the lead in providing feedback. The shift may partly be due to Oliver attending to the perceived task of the project and partly to this being the first occasion Oliver felt he had much to say. There is only a hint, at this point, that the shift is an issue for Taylor ("Well, not to defend myself, but I. . .").

The question of how much to discuss, and in what way, is a constant issue for an observer. The phrasing and tone of the feedback will determine how the process is perceived and how much a teacher can handle. In this conference, for example, Oliver must decide whether to note *all* of the events which might relate to context and continuity, or to select a few to discuss. Selecting issues to be discussed is a skill which an observer can develop during the feedback process, but initially it requires time-consuming, deliberative effort. One of the drawbacks of having conferences daily, often immediately after a class, was that Oliver had little or no time to contemplate how he might select and approach issues for discussion. As a result, to communicate to Taylor the relevance of the issues Oliver selected to discuss, their connection to context and continuity had to be made explicit. Oliver made some very explicit connections between incidents in the lesson and the issue of conceptual continuity (e.g., 19 and 23), but some of the more obscure items of discussion were not adequately connected to the issue of intellectual continuity. When implicit connections are not made explicit there is a danger of the observer's comments being perceived as arbitrary complaints.

Monday, Day 3
Different Perspectives on Success

> This episode illustrates the importance of ensuring feedback is clear and specific. Note that Oliver's comments about the microscopes are not explicitly connected to the issue of intellectual continuity for the students. More generally, the episode highlights how integral a thorough understanding of the nature of the subject matter is to giving feedback and to talking about the feedback process.

Class

49 **T**   *I worked really hard on my share of the Spring Festival. It is over now so I am going to give you a lot more attention than I have been over the last week or two.*

Taylor explicitly laid out the tasks for the lesson which were (1) to become familiar with the use of the microscope as a tool for learning about cells; and (2) to learn how to draw what is observed under the microscope. Students were given prepared slides of a multicellular leaf section and a single-cell animal (paramecium). During the lesson (ten minutes short because of an assembly) Taylor moved around the room and worked with students. Most of the students started with the plant cell and did not have time to look at the paramecium.

Conference

Taylor felt reasonably comfortable with the way class had gone, but Oliver was concerned that students had not accomplished as much as Taylor thought. He encouraged Taylor to look at some of the details of what had happened.

50 **T**   *A lot of late nights [with] Spring Festival last week. I'm pooped, really pooped. . . . And I still accomplished what I wanted them to accomplish. I laid [it] out on the board when we started. What I wanted them to do was to become familiar with the microscope . . . and coupled with that, I wanted them to learn to draw the diagrams, to keep a record of what they saw. . . . Those were my objectives. They were met. The only thing, of course, it was a short day. . . .*

Oliver was curious as to why Taylor had used both a paramecium *and* a leaf slide since the original plan, developed a week and a half earlier, called for using only the ciliated paramecium. The original reasoning was that observing a single-celled, ciliated organism would be the first of a series of steps toward understanding the structure and function of ciliated epithelial cells in lung tissue and what happens to those cells when they become cancerous. The point was to try to maintain a degree of visual and conceptual continuity between what students were viewing and what they were to learn about cells and cancer. The following are excerpts from the conversation:

51   **O**   *You used paramecium which is directly related to what you are going to do tomorrow and we will have a good look at it and the difference [between prepared slides and live paramecia] tomorrow. The things will be moving, including the cilia which you wanted them to see. But the leaf, why did you bring the leaf into it?*

52   **T**   *I don't know, I just decided that. . . .*

53   **O**   *The point is, what does the leaf have to do with cancer?*

54   **T**   *Nothing. . . . And even more ironic, little Alden drew the leaf first so that he only had time to do one [type of cell]. That [leaf] is all they have done. So there was less continuity.*

For the observer the introduction of the leaf cell was set within the broader issue of continuity. Oliver noted that Monday's work with the microscope had not been explicitly connected to the previous Friday's (Day 2) discussion about cases of cancer. This is the kind of disconnectedness that contributes to some students' difficulty in understanding the "broad picture" of what they are doing, and to their treatment of information and activities as discrete, episodic events. In the following excerpts it would seem that Oliver and Taylor were misunderstanding each other. Taylor interpreted Oliver's remarks on continuity as referring to management:

55   **O**   *I thought there was some pedagogical flatness there today. Not enough [of] telling them why they are doing these kinds of things. . . .*

56   **T**   *There were only two reasons why they were doing it, and I told them. . . . They did the things that I wanted them to do . . . and, you know, [it went] better than it has in the past sometimes, too. . . . I have, in the past, found microscope covers with spittle on them in the garbage, so it doesn't always go this smoothly. . . .*

Lack of clarity and specificity in feedback can result in an issue being blown out of proportion. In the above interchange, it was not clear that Oliver was talking about the need for an explicit connection between Friday's and Monday's work. He could have avoided this miscommunication by raising the issue of continuity directly or by providing an instance of what he meant.

At this point Oliver diverted the conversation to talk about an underlying tension in the feedback process (of which more will be said later):

57 **O** *It is fascinating when you and I sit down and do this because I would do it differently, just as you would do things that I do differently. In trying to be objective . . . it takes everything that I have got to sit back and watch because I want to do it my way, just as if you were in my position, you would want to do it your way. . . . I would probably suggest to you that when you look at the end point, the resultant diagram and what the kids understand — [and look at] the way you do it, which I would characterize as being looser, more free, than the way I would do it, which would be more structured, and more rigid — probably there is not that much difference between the two [end results].*

However, in the following excerpts Oliver shifts back, this time explicitly, to the issue of continuity between Monday's lab with the microscopes and Friday's discussion of cancer:

58 **O** *It is interesting, you know, after you and I just talked briefly at the end of the class and you read my notes, I was interested in trying to find out what the students had perceived. So I grabbed Steve because he was right beside me. I said to Steve, "Why are you doing this today?" and Steve said, "We are studying cells, you have to look at them, look and see what they look like." And I said, "Why?" and he said, "That is what we are supposed to do."*

59 **T** *That is typical of what you are going to get.*

60 **O** *So I tried to push him a little bit more and I asked, "What relationship does this class today bear to the two previous classes?" and he said, "Well, we are studying cancer." I mean, he was like [snaps fingers] with the responses and I said, "Why are you doing this in relationship with cancer?" He said, "I think what we are supposed to do is look at normal cells, and then we will be looking at abnormal cells." I thought that was terrific.*

61 **T** *That is good, because I hadn't said that to them.*

62 **O** *No, and he drew that together. That really made me feel good that he had perceived that your event today was a part of a continuum although you didn't refer to it. Now, Steve is sharp. The question that I asked is, do the other kids in the class have the same kind of understanding? And, that is something that you should ask yourself; and whether or not, in your strategy for dealing with a continuum, you want to make that more obvious or leave it the way it is.*

After several interchanges Taylor thought out loud about how he intended to structure the next several lessons. The issue of continuity was clearly part of his planning. It is important to note that, as he planned, he took into account the blocks of time he had to work within.

63 **T** *Now, in fact I am wondering whether I should push [the film] back because, you know, they are doing presentations on Wednesday. So half of the class*

*is taken with their presentations, and it would basically be the film with
no introduction, and no follow-up because it fills the time slot. I don't think
that is the way to use that film. . . . Probably what I am going to do is say,
"Here is the normal cell. You have seen some normal cells and I have given
you some correlation between the things you saw and what they are supposed to be doing under normal circumstances. Tomorrow I have a film for you
from the Cancer Society that is going to tell you about some of the differences
between the normal cell and the cancer cell." And I would assume that it
is going to fall into kind of a logical sequence for them.*

In the remaining few minutes of the conference Oliver brought up his (and Taylor's)
observation that the microscopes were dirty, and his concern that students might not
be able to see the very structures important for understanding the differences between normal and cancerous cells. Midway through the lab Taylor had given students
lens tissue to clean the scopes and he had instructed them in putting the microscopes
away.

64   **O**   *Some kids [were] actually looking through the microscope and searching
for information, trying to get meaning from it; and, as you showed me, the microscopes are in God awful shape. They are dirty. The slides are terrible. . . .*

65   **T**   *I got the feeling as the period was winding on, that that was what was happening. I found myself sort of suggesting to them, this is really bad, this
is really dirty. . . . A lot of classes have been using [the microscopes] but
they haven't been taking care of them. I am really concerned about these
microscopes.*

66   **O**   *Fair enough. I am glad to hear you say that you are going to look at them
ahead of time.*

67   **T**   *No, I am saying I didn't have a look at them ahead of time, which I should
have done. What I am saying is I think that maybe I found myself in one
of those teachable moments where there was a lesson to be learned from these
dirty microscopes.*

The conference was closed with comments about the next day's lesson:

68   **O**   *Okay, so your basic objective tomorrow then is to prepare a wet mount and
have them see what a paramecium looks like.*

69   **T**   *And in fact this attends to your concern about [students seeing for
themselves]. Now I can convince them that they are looking at living cells. . . .*

70   **O**   *And the other thing that you can do tomorrow, if you choose to do it, is
something that we talked about earlier. The reason that we got paramecia
is because they are ciliated, and the whole idea is to look at cilia as a means
of movement and hopefully to be able to then look at a ciliated epithelium
when we start talking about moving things out of the lungs.*

Considerations

It is commonplace that a teacher may not always be able to articulate, at the time, why she or he has done something in a particular way. Yet it is also generally agreed that this does not necessarily mean that there were no reasons, or for that matter, good reasons for a particular action. (Which, of course, leaves open the question of whether an action was the most appropriate to take.) Given the prior discussion about the use of a ciliated organism in this lab, it is understandable that Oliver was taken aback when a leaf cell was introduced into the lesson and perplexed when Taylor did not articulate a reason for doing so. (Why the event was significant, beyond the issues of context and continuity, will be dealt with later in the account.) In the following "Considerations" I sketch a plausible context for understanding Taylor's actions.

One theme that runs through this account concerns the hectic and demanding professional life of any teacher working with young people in a public school setting. Contributing to the stresses of intense contact with class after class of students are professional expectations which lie outside the formal demands of teaching (e.g., committee work, extra-curricular coaching, supervising student clubs and newspapers, and organizing major events). Such expectations are usually not written into a teacher's contract but they are very real and a teacher is under considerable pressure to carry her or his load (although what constitutes a reasonable load is hardly ever clear). One of the functions of established habits and routines in the classroom is to allow the teacher to conduct formal teaching activities when other aspects of professional or personal life are particularly demanding. Thus, it is probably seldom the case that an experienced teacher goes into a classroom "unprepared," but, in times of heavy extra-curricular demands, the preparation may be embodied, so to speak, in habits and routines which represent years of accumulated preparation and experience.

The intensity of classroom life itself is frequently stressful, and this can be particularly true during a laboratory exercise where various activities have to take place (students getting microscopes, setting them up, obtaining slides, etc.) before the class can even come to the substantive point of the exercise. From the teacher's perspective, the logistical complexities of a lab exercise have to be overcome with some degree of efficiency — and with an overriding concern for the safety of students and the care of expensive equipment — if the conceptual issues are to be made clear. The combination of logistical difficulties, and students who do not fully understand what they are to do or why they are doing it, can result in a relatively unstable classroom situation. Consequently, the "bells and whistles" of the laboratory are at once a boon and a curse to a science teacher. The motivational value of "hands on" involvement is sometimes diminished by the stressful conditions under which that involvement takes place.

Given that lab work can be fraught with pitfalls, it follows that a teacher would be inclined to rely on time-tested routines when extra-curricular demands are heavy. In Taylor's situation it is important to look at three aspects of routine. One is that the microscopic examination of both a plant and animal cell is a very common exercise (almost to the point of pedagogical tradition) in the study of the cell. Examination of only an animal cell represents a real departure from that tradition, and from Taylor's established routine. Second, the plant cell is frequently examined first because it has a thick cell wall and tends to be easier to see for beginners. Finally, no teacher wants to run out of material during a lesson and this is particularly true in a lab. During the conference, Taylor indicated his wish for the students to have more than one cell to examine and this may have been to avoid having rambunctious students left with nothing to do.

These are relevant features of context that likely contributed to Taylor's choices and actions, in spite of previous planning. A teacher's expression of satisfaction about a lesson often incorporates such context which, if fully explicated, might read something like, "I thought it went well, given (1) the explosive potential of these students; (2) the logistics of microscope labs; (3) the amount of prep time I had; and (4) how this exercise has gone in the past." Thus a teacher's sense of accomplishment involves a variety of factors, taken together. Sometimes, especially under complex and demanding conditions, a teacher's sense of success hinges on whether an event was brought to a satisfactory conclusion or *happened at all*, let alone how well it was executed.

The context determining an observer's sense of success is usually different. An observer is able to focus on one aspect of teaching (in this case, the issues of context and continuity) because she or he is free of personal and immediate involvement in the teaching act, and because she or he lacks a personal-historical sense of the situation. Consequently, a teacher's sense of success may at times be holistic and past-referenced, while an observer's is likely to be guided by images of how well the present lesson might have been conducted, *given the particular focus of the study*. These differing sets of implicit criteria allow a teacher to feel that everything went relatively well, and an observer to feel that things could have gone better. Explicitly discussing both sets of criteria might be one way of neutralizing the potential of sub rosa confrontation, and would be a step toward honouring the legitimacy of different stances.

Oliver explicitly acknowledged an instance of his and Taylor's different stances when he expressed his view of the differences in their teaching styles (57). This perceived difference was an issue which concerned Oliver throughout much of the case study. Oliver likely entered into dialogue with Taylor carrying images of how he might have handled various situations. The historical relationship between the two (Oliver as mentor) and Oliver's role as department head, made it difficult for him to adopt a strictly observational role. Such a role would entail no more and no less than reporting what he saw as it related to a given issue, engaging in substantive dialogue with the teacher (understanding reasons for the situation from the teacher's point of view), and allowing the teacher to deal with the feedback as he or she saw fit. As an authority in charge of the department, Oliver incorporated the expectations of the school and Board of Education. Such expectations are frequently implicit but a department head has the felt responsibility to represent them. So, for example, although Oliver was on leave from the school, he nevertheless keenly felt a department head's responsibility toward the care of equipment.

But, Oliver's concern about the dirty microscopes was not only the concern of a department head. It was substantively connected to the issue of intellectual continuity — it was important for students to practice using the scopes and to *see* the ciliated paramecia on the prepared slides so that they would know what to do and what to look for the next day when they observed live specimens with the cilia moving (a much more difficult task). And the *reason* for looking at the moving cilia of live paramecia was to engage the students in an interesting *activity* related to a later film. In that film ciliated organisms like the paramecium would be compared with the ciliated epithelial cells of our lungs. (Those cells remove harmful particles from the lungs and are functionally damaged by cancerous conditions caused by smoking.) But these *reasons* and *connections* were not explicitly spelled out in the interchange between Oliver and Taylor about the scopes (64–67). Further, the tone of Oliver's comments about the microscopes (e.g., 64, "The microscopes are in God awful shape . . ."") indicates that his concern for the students' ability to see the data was mixed with his concern for the equipment. Both Oliver and Taylor agreed that the microscopes should be clean so that they could be used properly, but the semantics and syntax of Oliver's comment (66), "I am glad to hear you say that you are going to look at them ahead of time," strike a tone which resonates more strongly with his role as a department head than as a peer. The implicit mixed message runs the risk of having the process perceived as traditional supervision in a new, but paper thin, wrapping.

   An observer's tone, clarity, and specificity are significant because they ultimately shape a teacher's perception of the feedback process. The discerning use of such techniques shapes the quality of the entire experience for both the teacher and observer. The effect of Oliver's tone can be understood in this light. In today's conference Oliver's comments tended to focus on the present rather than on what might be done to enhance continuity in the future. To some degree Oliver could have shifted the conversation to planning-for-the-future to help avoid a tone of blame-for-the-past.

Tuesday, Day 4

Being Explicit About the Process

The difficulty of the lab activity contributes to disruptions which are the focus of the conference. Oliver takes an important step in talking directly about the feedback process itself. This leads to insights about a teacher's personal high and low points which must be taken into account if an observer is to provide constructive feedback. Feedback concerning Taylor's clear efforts to provide context and continuity gets lost in the shuffle. However, the conference ends on a positive note with mutual and supportive planning.

Class

The central task for this lesson was for students to look at a live specimen of a ciliated paramecium. Taylor began the class by explicitly connecting this day's work to their discussions and activities at the beginning of the unit:

71 **T** *Now, what we are going to do today for microscopy is look at some live specimens. We have two types of specimens here. . . . One is the cell type that you were looking at yesterday which is paramecium. The other one is called spirostomum. . . . These are both a single cell. I guess the real reason for having two is because I worry that if the lesson doesn't go very well, if one of them becomes dead, one is a backup for the other. But I have a couple of reasons for doing this today. One is for you to practice your microscopy talents. . . . OK, later on I am going to want you to look at things like normal lung cells, cancerous lung cells, and I am no longer going to be expecting you to be learning to use the microscope. I want you to be fairly good at it so the thing that you are doing is making the cell comparisons. . . .*

[Finally,] back to the reading, the case study that we did, and our interest in cancer, specifically lung cancer and all of those things — [all are related to] the fact that the article talked about ciliated cells. Cilia, according to the article, are hair-like projections around a cell, in your throat, in your nasal passages . . . and these hairs sweep the dirt that you inhale back out of your lungs, back out of your wind pipe. The final result of that, of course, is when you blow your nose. You get rid of all the dirt that has accumulated in the mucus. It is like a filter, that is right, only it is better than a filter because it doesn't just stop the dirt, it moves it back out, OK, and one of the things

we are going to look at with the cancer cells is what happens to the cells'
ability to do their normal jobs. I think at one point last week we made the
reference to the point that the lung cells and the cells of the respiratory system
just don't do anything anymore and a person dies of pneumonia. That was
before class that we were talking about that. It wasn't here. . . . What I want
you to do here, specifically, is try and see the cilia on the paramecium. . . .
I am interested in the paramecium because hopefully what you will be able
to see are little hairs because paramecium is a single celled organism that
uses the hair-like projections to move. . . .

Taylor then made it clear that students were to examine the paramecium first and
detailed the lab procedures they were to use in order to get the work done. The exercise of seeing live paramecium under a microscope, especially the movement of the
cilia, is extremely difficult. Although the organism can be seen under low power, the
cilia are too tiny to be seen at all. The cilia can be seen under high power, but the
organisms are usually moving so fast that they swim out of the field of vision. A common procedure is to slow down the paramecium by adding a viscous fluid to the slide,
but this is difficult and messy, and frequently stops all movement, destroying the
point of the activity. It is a "high risk" exercise, but is spectacular when it works.
This lesson was not free of the usual kinds of difficulties a biology teacher experiences,
as can be seen in these excerpts:

72 **S** *It is broken. I can't see a thing, sir.*

73 **T** *What is the problem here, Jim? It doesn't focus? Those are the air bubbles.*

74 **S** *Sir, how are you supposed to do this? They are little cells. . . .*

75 **S** *Sir, can I take this apart and clean it? It is all dirty. I am not seeing nothing.*

76 **T** *There are all kinds of little organisms moving along. They are really tiny*
under lower power but see those little things skimming along? OK, be with
you in a second, Jim. . . .

77 **S** *On high power you can't see nothing.*

78 **S** *So what do we do now, sir?*

79 **T** *I want you to try and see the hair-like projections that the paramecium moves*
with, which means that you have to go right up to high power. . . .

80 **S** *Sir, are these germs? I can't see nothing. . . .*

81 **S** *I can't see nothing at high power.*

82 **S** *Do we have to draw this?*

83 **S** *Sir, we can't see anything. . . .*

84   **T**   *Now remember what I told you about the field of view. . . . When you were looking at the paramecia under low power you had all this area to look at under the slide, and you saw these little guys scooting around. What you have done now by going to high power is you are only looking at a small piece which makes the whole thing bigger. This small area now takes up the same field which means it is magnified. So you have to basically move this slide around until you can find one of these little guys and of course they are moving faster than you are moving the slide. It is a trial and error thing.*

The last statement by Taylor was important because it began to establish the pedagogical context of the task by helping the students understand reasons for their lack of success. Later he continued to develop this context:

85   **S**   *We found one, sir!*

86   **T**   *Good. Is it moving still?*

87   **S**   *It is gone now.*

88   **T**   *I have a means to slow these guys down, just like it is harder for you to run through water than it is for you to run through air. We had that discussion once. It is harder for these guys to swim if they are in a different substance that is thicker, and the thicker substance that I have is called methyl cellulose. Now, there are two ways that you can apply the methyl cellulose. . . .*

However, if the exercise was frustrating for the students, it was no less so for Taylor.

89   **T**   *OK, we have got to talk. We have got a couple of things that we have to talk about. . . . A lot of people here didn't get very much done today, and it has to do with the fact that you are treating this class like recess. Whether it be the hitting or the joking or the insults, it is not appropriate in here. . . .*

He then reiterated the reason why having clean microscopes was essential and acknowledged the difficulty of the task, while reminding them of why it was important that they see the cilia.

90   **T**   *You have been conditioned to believe what the teacher says, to provide what the teacher wants. That is great for getting through school. It is not good science. As scientists leaving this room today you should be very unconvinced. . . . Some of you saw living single cells, OK, but what about cilia? You should still be unconvinced because you haven't seen them yet. Remember away back in February we talked about direct evidence. And really to establish a fact, you need direct evidence. Most of you would probably accept as direct evidence the fact that you looked through the microscope and you saw them, but most of you haven't seen [the cilia] so you are working without direct evidence, and you should have the amount of doubt that goes with that. I don't know*

to what degree it is worth going back because I am wondering here whether we are limited by the microscopes, the size and speed of these little guys, how much the microscope will magnify them, how clearly you can see through the microscope. I will fiddle with these things tomorrow morning; if I can find something that represents cilia, I will keep it on the slide for period two. If I can't, I think we have to move on. It seems to me that also you just need more time at the microscopes. But the other thing that is pulling at me, of course, is [while] some of you need more time at the microscopes to find them, there are the same number of people who are bored and they are ready to start horsing around again so it is kind of an impasse. . . .

Conference

The dominant theme of this conference, introduced by Taylor, concerned the behaviour of some of the students during the lesson. The issue sparked conversation about Taylor's immediate state of mind with respect to the class, more general issues concerning his views about teaching, and the substance of the lesson.

91 **T** *You know that I run the class very loosely and you do things differently and may have the same result. I think today what has happened is they have exceeded my patience. It has gone too far [for] a combination of reasons: partly because I think they are used to being in the classroom. Partly because [of their recent trip to] the zoo, big high, big outing, cancer, really interesting, microscopes, and just kind of settling down. Beth sat there all period. She hasn't even been in school for five days and she sat there and told me she was bored. You know, she is being perverse because she got into a lot of trouble with the vice-principal. But it is representative of what is happening in the whole room. It is basically that now they want to fool around. And it is also a reflection of the way I manage the classroom that they can get into that situation. It happened to be a day when [I had] really low energy, really bad. It was a bad night. It was a bad morning. I had no energy. I had a splitting headache. Usually when I feel like this there are two things that happen: I go berserk at them or let it run its course and talk about it after.*

Oliver asked Taylor if, in retrospect, there was anything he would have done differently and, from the standpoint of the feedback process, Taylor's initial comments are important to heed. Continuing on from Oliver's comments the previous day (page 33) on their different ways of conducting classes, Taylor begins to examine his own teaching style:

92 **T** *Well you know, I think one can run it a little tighter. If [the lesson] works it is fine, if it doesn't work, one starts to ask all these questions. It is like any postmortem. . . . It was the same in period four. . . . I was going for the same thing, which was, you know, to have a chance to float around; go to each individual person and talk about what they see. Of course, the trouble was they didn't see anything. It is a chronic problem with this lab. [You and I] didn't talk about it before, but it is. We found that, too, these are not the* *best microscopes. It doesn't help that it is spring, second term. [By now a microscope] is supposed to have been well used and used hard. Twenty minutes into the class, Bill comes and asks me to take a look at the lenses and they are offset so that he can't focus. He can't see anything.*

After some further discussion about the condition of the microscopes, Oliver suggested the possibility of students cleaning them in class, as a way of saving time. This was met with some ambivalence and Taylor pointed out that because the scopes were so dirty the task was not an easy one.

Oliver turned to the feedback process itself:

93   **O**   *I sat down last night and thought about what we had said yesterday and I want to talk a little bit about the [feedback] process if you feel comfortable with that. If you don't, that is fine too. It was nice to get your phone call last night. It was nice. I really appreciated that, and then, after that, I sat down and kind of tried to think over what we were doing. I got the feeling yesterday, because my comments are starting to get quite direct, . . . that I was putting you on the defensive, and that is natural in this kind of situation. What I am trying to do is, when I see what I conceive to be issues, as I perceive them, I bring them to your attention; they may or may not be issues for you.*

Such a move was very much on Oliver's mind as is evident in his comment to the researcher on the previous day: "So I guess the question I have to ask myself tomorrow is, you know, do I go back and revisit it again after Taylor has had some time to think and after I have had some time to think, or do I just take and put that one aside and start, not afresh, but being a little more cautious as to what I am bringing to his attention. I don't know." As the excerpts from Taylor's reply show, the comment about the process stimulated a number of introspective thoughts concerning his view of himself as a teacher and the relationship he had with a difficult class. These are important because they contributed to Oliver's understanding of the situation:

94   **T**   *Being on the defensive doesn't imply any threat because, of course, you can defend your point of view. . . . As far as this day goes, there is nothing threatening. . . . Let's face it, we lost the game today. But there are eighty-five games to the season right, and you don't win them all, and that is exactly the way I feel about this class. . . . There are so many things that are eating at me in addition to the fact that I am overtired. . . . I am run down now. But I will tell you if they had been horsing around like that on Friday we would have been right back to task. You do peak, you do cycle, and it is like that, you know. You just have to get out of the rut, just get out of the rut, because they sense it as a group. Steve, Jim, and those people, they are horsing around today because they know that I am low on energy and they can get away with it. And the only thing I think we can do, and I have done it in the past, I mean, I have actually gone berserk, like I said, really mad, you know, and then they are always cool toward me because they don't like the fact that I act so violently. The other thing is what I did today, which is to lay it on*

the line, which is to simply say, "I really can't put up with that, I don't like it," and approach it maturely, as opposed to emotionally. I must admit I hate kicking people out of class. . . . I hate losing anybody. I have only got them for an hour. So that puts some limitations on me too because by this point in the year they have figured me out. They know I am not going to kick — well, once I kicked a couple of people out of period four, but I have never kicked anybody out of here. So even when I say it is unacceptable, they really know that all I am going to do is steer them back, but I am never going to act on any power or discipline. I am really trying to use the strength of my character to keep them in line, and on a low day like today you see it all coming out. Because without the strength, the character, without the personality to keep them in line, there is nothing holding them back.

As the conversation turned toward the nature of the student interaction, Oliver adopted a way of speaking which allowed for perceptions to be corroborated by Taylor.

95   **O**   *It seemed to me from your discussion [with the class], as I was listening to it, and was taking notes, that it was more important to you to nip the idea of insults because it seemed, again, if I interpreted you correctly, there was a much larger proportion of insults going on amongst the members of the group and it was more widespread, hence your comment about insults. I thought that was very well put. As you say, it was mature, but you said very clearly, "It is not appropriate; I want it to stop because it takes priority over learning and learning is the thing that we are here to do," and, you were very hard on that point. . . .*

Another feature of the complicated life of a classroom teacher can be seen in the conversation about Steve.

96   **T**   *Steve was one of the main people I was addressing because Steve really has a tongue. He was insulting today. . . .*

97   **O**   *Is it worth talking to Steve one-on-one?*

98   **T**   *You know, it was so much easier with the six period day. We did a lot of talking to the students. You lose those moments. They have got one spare. He doesn't have a spare, period three. . . . And these kids don't come by after school. I have tried it. . . . I mean it is difficult and right now, let's face it, it is logistics. At the beginning of the period I want them all together and they all want to chat with me, so if I try and have a talk with Steve, it is going to be Steve and a bunch. Maybe the beginning of the period is the only time. After the period you and I are talking. All of a sudden you get into a situation where it is hard talking to a kid on a one-to-one basis, the way things are set up now. It is difficult.*

Within the context of the discussion about classroom behaviour Taylor commented on the nature of the lesson itself, and this led to a possible resolution to the problem.

99   **T**   *Intellectually, this lesson was almost set up for failure. We can't get out of the lesson what on paper seems so super. Yesterday we talked of . . . continuity. I had my doubts then but I didn't realize [the lack of success] was going to be so total. I figured only a couple of people might get it. [The paramecia] would be dead by the time they slowed down enough for us to look at them so we don't see cilia movement. I was realizing half way through the period that that was the way it was going to go.*

100   **O**   *OK, can I suggest a couple of ways that might help?* [Oliver makes two technical suggestions on how to slow down the organisms so they can be seen.]

101   **T**   *We can't show them the cilia first hand unless they can see it under the microscope. So I think what . . . I might do is set up my own microscope in period four because it is bugging me and I want to get onto it as soon as possible. If it turns out it is a difference between my expertise and theirs, then fine, "Come over here, I have found it," fair enough.*

102   **O**   *That is a good strategy.*

103   **T**   *And also if it does turn out that it is a matter of expertise, then at least I have that back up for the class and probably now — and it is the first time I ever thought about it — now that I think about it, I should have been doing that on a regular basis; setting up my own work as a back up in terms of technique.*

The discussion turned to planning for the next lesson. Here it is important to note that Taylor provided further insight into the logistical impediments in his situation. Oliver offered concrete support and the conference ended on an upbeat, and co-operative, note:

104   **T**   *It all comes down to the time. How much you can prepare? How much you can follow-up? I have got stuff to give them back that should be marked. . . . But still there are all kinds of other things that come up like classroom management and then there is all the follow-up. Isn't this neat the way it was done? — the preparation and the follow-up — but you look at a whole unit of work and you are talking about a job, a day-in and day-out job with all kinds of distractions. The fact that I had to go down to the office and talk to Bill Wilfred about a purchase order number. He was having trouble with it. It had my name on it. To me that is a distraction because that is not what I am here for. I am not an administrator. I have a filefolder of purchase orders. And it all takes away from the classroom teaching, and that is the time that I would have spent getting organized today. Getting the film loop out, looking at it, making sure. . . . I keep thinking to myself, you know, any day now I have got to sit down and I have got to spend an hour on preparation and that is terrible. I shouldn't be in that situation. . . .*

105   **O**   *I am just wondering if you are able to get one specimen underneath the*

microscope, even one, under one of the good mics tomorrow, if you had the cilia film loop, you might be able to pull that together. . . . Maybe this afternoon I can have a fast look in AV and see if there is any film material there which . . .

106 **T**   *There is a film on the paramecium . . .*

107 **O**   *Yeah, OK, is it worth . . .*

108 **T**   *I think, yes, just off the top of my head, I am going to have to look it up. I may be wrong . . .*

109 **O**   *Well, leave it to me. . . . We are learning. Why don't we cut it there . . .*

110 **T**   *You know what is the beauty of this, because this is an ongoing course . . . from the beginning. I have taught this course now for nine years straight. What this is doing for us is it is getting down on paper all the things that we think about; and we experience them again the next year with all this to look at.*

Considerations

As an observer, Oliver has two interconnected functions related to feedback. The first concerns the *substance* of feedback, and entails helping the teacher analyze specific moves made in teaching in terms of the focal issues (context and continuity). The second involves explicitly reflecting, where appropriate, on the feedback *process*.

With regard to substance, even though Taylor addressed the issues of context and continuity during today's lesson, neither instance was mentioned during the conference. At the start Taylor addressed conceptual continuity (71) by talking about the relationship between what the students were doing on that day and what they had done previously. Later he addressed pedagogical context (84) when he explained to the students why they were unable to see the cilia of the paramecium. Both of these instances were noteworthy and merited attention.

Oliver did, however, explicitly introduce the issue of the feedback process (93), but he did not firmly or explicitly anchor the talk about process to a reminder of the substantive function of feedback. Such a connection was likely warranted at this point.

The ability to talk elegantly, appropriately, and with integrity about the various facets of feedback — integrating process and substance — is a skill that an observer must cultivate, just as a teacher might work on making integrative connections for the students by providing substantive and pedagogical reasons for classroom happenings. For instance, in this project it is assumed that the various parts of teaching (subject matter, management, interaction, etc.) are complexly interconnected. Feedback on any part should heed the relationship of that part to the whole.

Meaning and *control*, to cite two parts of teaching, are not isolated — if students cannot do what they have been asked to do, or if they cannot make sense of that which they are to comprehend, then it might be expected that, in proportion to their frustration, they will engage in activities which are counter productive to learning. Taylor tacitly recognized the interconnections between control and substance when he said, "this lesson was almost set up for failure" (99). This may have been an opportunity for Oliver to revisit specific details of the lesson (positive and negative) within the context of an explicit reminder of the focus on the substance and process of feedback.

Speculation as to why Oliver did not integrate Taylor's concerns into the substance and process of the conference is risky. But, it is worth remembering that, while Oliver is free from the immediacies of classroom teaching and can have a relatively narrow focus with regard to teaching, he is not free from the immediacy and complexity of observing the teaching process, nor of the resulting substance and interaction of the conference. Oliver may have ideas as to how the conference might go, or should go, but he must also respond to exigencies like, in this case, the teacher's initiation of, and concentration on, the issue of the students' behaviour. Under these conditions the integrative function of feedback may fade from view.

Earlier I noted that Taylor's criterion of success seemed to be holistic and past referenced (56, "It doesn't always go this smoothy"). Perhaps that is true when a lesson goes well in terms of classroom management. When there are disruptions his focus becomes specific (e.g., Steve) and present-referenced, at least with regard to management. In Taylor's case, reference to the present involves strong images of how people should treat one another (no insults, no punching, no ordering others around). These contribute to his own guide for treating his class (no bossing, control yourself). Considerable stress might be predicted for Taylor when individuals in the class do not honour these images.

Regardless of some of the snags in the conference, it ended on a very positive note with planning for the next lesson. Taylor's remark (110) is important because it suggests the potential of feedback for curriculum development.

Wednesday, Day 5

Co-operative Planning

This episode points to the need to relate specifics to the general intent of feedback. It also shows Oliver's sincere willingness to be concretely helpful. Notice the discontinuity between the theme of cells and cancer, and the presentation at the start of the lesson. Also note Taylor's use of the film loop to help students understand the broader context and reasons for their activities on Tuesday.

Class

The lesson had three parts: in the first part two students, Steve and Bill, presented a project on "Particles" and "States of Matter." The project was not related to the unit on cancer and the cell, but it was part of Taylor's program that each student or pair of students present a project during the term. These were always presented during the first half of the lesson on Wednesdays. The topics were chosen by the presenters, and the projects were evaluated by the class. Oliver did not comment on this phase of the lesson during the conference. (It might have been considered "off limits" since it was a classroom routine which was established well before Oliver's involvement with this particular unit.)

In the next portion of the lesson, Taylor acknowledged the previous day's problem with trying to see the live paramecium, and handed back and commented on the accuracy of their earlier drawings of cells. From the standpoint of context and continuity, Taylor gave reasons why he regarded accuracy as important. One reason concerned misinformation, the other was tied to the future work they would be doing. Here is a relevant excerpt:

111 **T** *For you, looking back to your diagram, six months from now, six weeks from now, having forgotten what the leaf looked like, it will jog your memory, but [if it is not accurate] it will jog your memory in a way that is not accurate. It will jog your memory about something that in fact wasn't there. You drew from a different reason other than recording accurately what you saw. It was too quickly filled in. . . . Now drawing accurately has got nothing to do with your artistic talent. It has nothing to do with whether or not you are a good artist, but the idea of whether the cell is like this, or whether it is like this with respect to its neighbour. . . . You see, the differences between a normal cell and a cancerous cell that we will be looking at later on may be such that if you are not careful about the way you draw the cells, by looking at the diagrams, the normal cell and cancerous cell, you are not going to be able to see any difference.*

In the final portion of the lesson Taylor showed a film loop and a short movie, both of which photographed moving cilia on paramecia. At the beginning and during the film loop he identified which aspects of the film the students should focus on:

112 **T**   *This is a film loop. . . . I just want to show you the paramecia on this represen-*
tation. Be aware of the fact that now I am not giving you direct evidence.
OK, of course what they are doing here is they are going through all the
parts [of the paramecium]. I am not really concerned with that at this point.
I want you to take a look at the action around here which, even at this size,
is difficult to see. So, of course, under the microscope, we were kind of set-
ting ourselves up for failure. . . . See, there? CILIA, which they use, of course,
for locomotion. Notice the rotation. . . . There, there is a good shot of the
cilia. See it? . . . So this loop is of limited value but at least I can show you
the cilia that I hoped you would see under the microscope. Let's see, when
you see the size of the cilia you realize why, perhaps, it was hard for you to see.

Taylor then talked about the issue of evidence in science and integrated characteristics of the pedagogical context within which the students were working:

113 **T**   *OK, so, is the film loop enough evidence for you? . . . Is this enough evidence*
for you [that paramecia have cilia]? . . . You see you are playing this kind
of tight rope where you are a student and you are working with a certain
type of facilities, but I am trying to get you to think as if you are scientists,
and you are looking at things empirically. Empirical means trying to
establish facts [through direct experience]. And of course we have got cer-
tain limitations in the school. Empirical observations or empirical discoveries
are . . . first hand discoveries that you make yourself. And I did want you
to discover empirically for yourself that paramecia have cilia. These little
hair-like projections that beat back and forth. To draw that — the thing that
made that difficult was time. A lot of people were getting to the end of the
period. How much time do I want to spend on this simple principle? Today,
tomorrow, the next day, or ten minutes. So, time is a problem that affects
your ability to do empirical work. Another thing of course is equipment or
technology. . . . Now, maybe if we could magnify it to the point where the
cilia were that big, then, yes, we would see cilia. The microscope doesn't
magnify that much. The lenses are not that powerful. The equipment limits
what we can do.

Conference

Taylor began the conference by talking about his feelings toward teaching at the moment and the professional context within which he worked:

114 **T**   *I think it is going to be very hard for us to say something positive. I am feel-*
ing very negative about the whole teaching process at this point. I am tired
of the students, and they are tired of me. But I find myself in the situation
now where so many other things seem to be taking priority over the actual

class, which is standard, which has happened often to you. It has happened to me before but since we formalized this kind of investigation, it needs to be attended to. Remember yesterday, when we were having our conversation, I said, you know, "We need some preparation time, desperately." Fortunately, I have enough material to cover, enough things to do in the class and yet I think a lot of the negative things and a lot of the less desirable things are a result of the fact that classroom teaching is no longer what it used to be. But the [Board of Education] and the school make more and more demands on time, to the point where I don't have any preparation time and it is getting ridiculous. Because a lot of it is, you know, stuff that, well, a lot of it I have taken on myself. It is back to that same old conversation of, "Well, next year I am going to try and take on less." Yeah, sure. It has been steadily more every year. That just doesn't work anymore. I wonder how to deal with that. I guess inevitably it is longer days. But, you know, this whole thing, to my mind, is what is the problem. It is a greater problem than how are you going to deal with Steve or what about those students at the back of the room. To my mind right now, maybe it is just the way I feel today, to my mind it is a larger problem. . . . I don't know what to do about it, I am just presenting that problem because I felt at some point I wanted to talk about it on the tape. Not that I am asking you for a solution to the problem. . . .

After discussion about management (following their presentation, Bill and Steve had not paid attention for the rest of the lesson), Oliver focussed on the issue of the students' drawings. As can be seen in the following excerpts, the point, as it relates to context and continuity, seems to get lost in the discussion.

115 **O**   *The other thing that I just want to push a little bit is, you did an analysis on the board with the kids as to your expectations with respect to accuracy and diagrams and you showed them the various problems that they had and, I think, clearly for me, indicated the areas of difficulty so that the message there was very clear. I wrote down here two things: is the evidence that you have got there, the difficulties that they seem to be having, a direct result from them not observing carefully enough; or are they observing carefully enough but not able to put the stuff on paper; or [do they not have] a clear and sufficient idea as to what you wanted and so, therefore, are not able to translate what they see to what they observe. So there are three possibilities there. Any reaction to that?*

Taylor pointed out that the drawing exercise and the feedback on it was not meant to be evaluative, but was the easiest way of finding out the students' weaknesses and addressing them.

116 **O**   *Well, I liked the way you pushed on the negative and then on the positive, ending on a higher note, saying, you know, you did a good job despite the fact you had difficulty here. Here was some of the good stuff that you did. But what I want to bring to your attention is, in terms of the issues of context and continuity and understanding the information, the negative things*

> *are the ones that we are most concerned about because it is an issue of look-*
> *ing at the material and drawing from that material evidence which you can*
> *then bring to bear on the issues as opposed to the positive which were more*
> *issues of drawing, you know, no shading, no ink. They did those kinds of*
> *things which are useful because in attempting to communicate to you what*
> *they know, those kind of cloud and get in the way. We all have this problem.*
> *I mean, it is not anything peculiar to you, it is the old thing of looking through*
> *the microscope and the kid says, "What am I supposed to see," and then you*
> *are supposed to see this. The whole thing. I don't know how to get around that.*

117 **T**   *I don't quite understand the problem that you are presenting. The problem*
> *is that of all the negative things?*

118 **O**   *No, I am not presenting a problem, it is just an observation more of the fact*
> *that you presented both sides which I really like. And the fact invariably*
> *that kids at this level have difficulty knowing what it is they are to put on*
> *paper.*

Toward the end of the above discussion it is clear that Taylor did not follow Oliver's
train of thought. The connection between what Oliver initially said and his last statement (118) is not clear, and the thrust of his original point, seemed to get lost.

Oliver then commented on Taylor's discussion about evidence.

119 **O**   *One of the things I liked [was your] talk about empirical stuff. . . . I thought*
> *that was really nice. The fact that now those students have a real sense that*
> *just because you see something on a film doesn't necessarily mean it is "true"*
> *— the whole idea of truth we won't get into — but it is not evidence in the*
> *true sense, the empirical sense that you were talking about. And that is nice.*

While Oliver addressed the substantive issue about evidence, he did not acknowledge
the further step that Taylor took when he tied the issue of evidence to the pedagogical
context of the situation and the students' failure (through little fault of their own)
to see cilia "first hand."

Taylor and Oliver then turned to future planning:

120 **T**   *OK, what I really wanted to do in this meeting — because that is where I*
> *am at right now, you know. You plan out five days and you go, go, go, and*
> *you say, "Day five, let me get all my material out and see where I am going."*
> *That is where I am at right now. Get the material out and look at the unit*
> *again and take a hard look. The hospital trip is still in limbo. I told you*
> *that yesterday. I phoned her back, she didn't phone me. I phoned back to-*
> *day. She hasn't phoned back. I am going to have to keep at her because she*
> *has got me down for the holiday Monday. . . .*

121 **O**   *Do you want to sit down tonight and have a look at this stuff and kind of*
> *get your head around it?*

At this point Taylor began to plan out loud. Oliver reminds him of the issue of continuity and offers assistance:

122 **T** *What I am saying, yeah, I don't know specifically, but what I want to do is — I have to make a decision. I think probably I want to do the cheek cell tomorrow, and after I have done the cheek cell, I want to do some cell physiology and I want to get to the nucleus. I want to get to the membrane and I want to do the dialysis experiment. I think that is the direction I am headed.*

123 **O** *One of the things that I just caution you to keep in mind, and it is something that I talked about right at the beginning, was the fact that we can't get away from the theme of cancer too much. . . . What I am saying, for the kids, remember the whole issues of context and continuity. If we go off into an awful lot on cells and don't talk about cancer — now you talked about cancer today, you know, you are bringing it back. But as long as whatever you do attends to the kind of overall thoughts about the unit on cancer so we don't go eight days without mentioning cancer and, finally, as the unit was put together, bang, on the eighth day you start talking about cancer.*

124 **T** *No, I understand what you are saying. . . . So I think I will keep that in mind with the dialysis. I have always done the dialysis experiment because it is an experiment and there is a considerable degree of success. . . . But it has got nothing to do with cancer. There is no part of the cancer that we can talk about I think.*

125 **O** *Well the other thing to do is to present them with a cancer cell. "This is a cancer cell, it is growing really fast, how does this stuff get in?" Play it that way. . . .*

126 **T** *And so I can tie it in there. You know, what you are doing there is, you are doing the application with the nutrients, and so on. So I think I have to sit down tonight and get it clear. Today represents the end of what I've thought out. . . . Fortunately I have been able to last through a certain number of days. I had a lot of other stuff to do outside of class time. . . .*

127 **O** *Is there anything I can help you with?*

128 **T** *I don't think so, because I have to be more definite of where I am going before I can say I need help with this or that.*

129 **O** *If tonight, for instance, you find you want some more stuff run-off and things like that, just let me know and I will. I can get a quick turnaround time down at the [head office] if you want things like photocopying and that sort of thing.*

130 **T** *I have learned a heck of a lot already. I have certainly learned a heck of a lot considering how many times I have taught this unit. . . .*

Considerations

Ideally, feedback should relate the specifics of teaching to students' learning and behaviour. In this case, for instance, it would be optimal if Taylor's efforts to provide context and continuity were rewarded with immediate and demonstrable effects; Oliver's job simply would be to help Taylor see the relationship between specific pedagogical moves and student outcomes. Classroom situations are seldom that straightforward, however. While Oliver and Taylor may profitably examine specific instances of teaching to see how Taylor provided context and continuity, it would be foolish to expect that in every instance there would be obvious "effects." This is not to give up on the idea that there is some effect on students as a result of providing relevant context and conceptual continuity from day to day — it is just to recognize that the "effect" is incremental and relatively long term. A teacher cannot change the personal history of a student's schooling, present expectations, attitude, or achievement, in a few hours, days or weeks, regardless of how well he or she teaches with respect to context and continuity.

Given the circumstances, Oliver and Taylor's work together assumes what Shulman has called a "normative" conception of effectiveness.[1] Rather than attending to, say, outcomes in terms of student achievement, their work is guided by normative images of what seems appropriate to do (with respect to context and continuity) given the situation. The paucity of data on immediate "effects" in teaching is all the more reason why the teacher and observer need to discuss episodes where there is fairly clear evidence that the teaching is consistent with the normative position agreed upon at the outset. Discussion should focus on the details of what was said and done so that the teacher can see the way in which it corresponds to normative guides. In other words, feedback should involve more than "strokes" when things go well.

There were two instances in this conference where Oliver could have focussed more on the details of teaching with respect to context and continuity. He praised Taylor's talk about evidence (119), but without attending to how it fit with context and continuity. A discussion could have elaborated on how Taylor was attempting to integrate the substantive point about evidence with the pedagogical context so that students would be more likely to realize what he was trying to do in the class and that failure was not due to their own ability. In a discussion Taylor and Oliver could have addressed whether and how the issue might have been clarified for the students.

Another opportunity to link teaching to context and continuity occurred early in the conference with the discussion about the diagrams. Oliver could have attended to Taylor's attempt to tie the importance of accurate drawings to the need to distinguish between normal and cancerous cells. What happened in the discussion about the diagrams (115–118) is not all that clear.

One interpretation of that series of interactions is that Oliver started with a valid point about the way in which the diagram issue was handled but, in an effort to not appear pejorative, qualified the issue to the extent that eventually the point was lost. Thus the discussion tended to emphasize the lack of clarity of Oliver's point rather than how the episode was or could have been handled. The interchange shows the importance of clarity during the conference. As a rule of thumb an observer can avoid an unnecessarily judgemental tone by dealing with concrete specifics, describing and analyzing the composition of events and their perceived relationship to the central issue, rather than talking in obtuse generalities. Such a stance might ease the way toward a more fruitful discussion between Oliver and Taylor — one which keeps an eye on the issues of context and continuity, recognizes that Taylor *has* addressed those issues, recognizes that those are not the only issues with which he must contend, and quickly and concretely moves to a discussion of what, if anything, should have been done differently.

---

1. L. Shulman, "Paradigms and Research Programs in the Study of Teaching: A Contemporary Perspective," in *Handbook of Research on Teaching,* ed. M. C. Wittrock, 3rd ed. (New York: MacMillan, 1986), pp. 3-36.

Thursday, Day 6
A Crisis with the Process

The lesson goes extremely well in terms of the theme of cancer and cell biology and in terms of making the necessary connections for the subject matter to be interesting and meaningful to students. The interaction between Oliver and Taylor is not as smooth and brings out underlying personal stresses as well as those related to the feedback process.

Class

The occurrences of this day can be seen as a crisis with respect to the feedback process, but that becomes apparent only in the context of later events. Taylor's initial plan was to have the lesson in two parts. In the first part he would project a normal and a cancerous cell, side-by-side, on a screen and have students draw a diagram of each and answer several questions on a prepared sheet (e.g., "Explain how cancer cells differ in structure from normal cells"). In the second part of the lesson students were to observe a film from the Cancer Society called "From One Cell," and answer a series of prepared questions.

It is not too clear how it happened, but Taylor apparently expected Oliver to bring, from another school, the prepared slides of normal and cancerous cells needed for the first part of the lesson. Oliver was not informed about this and was surprised when Taylor asked for the slides. After a quick strategic huddle, the two parts of the lesson were switched. This gave Oliver time to drive to the other school and obtain the slides.

Given the new plan, the class proceeded very smoothly. To give a sense of the interaction, here is a sketch of the comparison conducted between normal and cancerous cells which were projected on a screen:

131 **T**   *OK, everybody got all of those [questions] answered? Lets go on to the next set of sheets. I want to take a look at them in some detail. I think the film finished off just where we wanted to get going. Steve, please put the cards away. You are going to have to do a diagram here, but if you haven't got a pencil, a pen will be fine. I think I can supply you with pencils. I have some pencils. Do you need a pencil? I guess we are going to have to turn the lights on. Just let me check and see how well we can look at these. I will turn one light on. Now, first of all I want to tell you that the one on the left is the normal cell. The one on the right is the cancerous cell. I didn't get*

myself the question sheets. Just a moment. Notice on your sheet it says "Question one." First of all, note the pink stained cells are the older cells, while the blue stained cells are the younger, immature cells, OK? And underneath there, large enough to fill the space, I would like you to draw the two types. Keep in mind the kinds of suggestions I gave you about drawing when I gave you back your diagrams yesterday? Yes?

132 **S** *Do you want us to draw the whole cell? Just one cell or the whole picture?*

133 **T** *You are better off to draw one cell in detail than you are to draw the whole thing as a very sketchy representation. Pick a cell that you feel represents — obviously the one in the middle on the left seems like the logical one to draw for one of the pink ones. But on the right hand side pick one that you feel is a good representation of the cell because you will notice that it says for the diagram, a normal cell, not the slide of cells, OK? Now, these cells are cells that were taken in a pap test. I am reading this. This comes with the slide that I brought for you. The one on the left. Normal cells taken in a pap test. How many people here know what a pap test is? Right, I think I have to explain that. . . . [Taylor explains a pap test.] It is a common cancer site in women. When we talk about types of cancer, what causes cancer, I will come back to this specific type of cancer and talk about it in more detail. But the point is, a pap test is essentially a biopsy. I told you what a biopsy was last Friday. Who recalls what a biopsy is?*

134 **S** *A test or something.*

135 **T** *It is an examination. It is [the removal of tissue which is then examined] for cancer. It is the only absolute test for cancer. You look at the cells and see if they are cancerous. . . .*

Taylor and the students continued to compare the two slides in an effort to understand the characteristics of cancerous cells. The task was complicated by the fact that the magnification was different for the two prepared slides. In the following, notice how Taylor wove into the discussion the reasons why understanding these characteristics were important:

136 **T** *So, if you scale up the one on the right or you scale down the one on the left, do you think the blue cells are the same size? Do you think the cancer cells are the same size?*

137 **S** *No, they look like they are joined. They are one.*

138 **T** *That could be because they are lying on top of each other in the slide. It could also be because they are in the process of dividing. That could be the reason they are stuck together. You can't tell from the slide. But one thing that is interesting to note is how much cytoplasm there is in a normal cell. We will compare young cells so that we know it is not because they are young. There is a normal young cell. Notice the amount of cytoplasm compared to the*

amount of nucleus. Look at the amount of cytoplasm and the amount of nucleus in these cells. How would you compare the amount of volume taken up by the nucleus compared to the amount of volume taken up by the cytoplasm? What has more volume in the cancer cell?

139 **S**   *The nucleus.*

140 **T**   *The nucleus, OK. If you were going to talk about ratios, the ratio of the nucleus to the cytoplasm is smaller in a normal cell and is larger in a cancer cell. These are all the kinds of things that a lab technician would use to identify a cancer cell because — now stop and think of the responsibility, OK? You take a six month technician's course or a year technician's course at a technical college then you go off working for a lab, either a lab in a hospital like General or a lab in an independent clinic that routinely takes in tons and tons of these tests from doctors, processes them and sends them back out. Now you have got a heck of a big responsibility because you are sitting down at your microscope and you have a whole basket full of slides and you have to finish these ones before lunch, and then go off on your lunch break. You pull out the specimen. You put it under the microscope. You are looking at slides now. Now, you as a technician have got to make a trained decision. With this person, am I looking at cancer cells, or am I looking at normal cells? Because if I am looking at normal cells, that is a heck of a responsibility to make sure the person knows that. If the person has cancer, that is a heck of a responsibility to make sure you don't call those cells normal. . . .*

Conference

Taylor and Oliver both agreed that it was a very good class, in spite of the rough start. During the discussion Taylor indicated that some of his anxiety was due to the fact that his house had just been robbed.

141 **T**   *In the beginning I was frustrated. I've got all that background frustration of the robbery, of having the police come over late last night, getting up late this morning. I went home last night with a real basic priority which was to get on track and to get my momentum back after being so tired. This has been a flat week for me as a person and as a teacher, and, of course, this all negated my sitting down and applying myself to marking, which basically is my way to get organized. It is a great feeling to have everything marked. It takes the pressure off, and releases stress, and I didn't get it done last night. And, I know that part of it was the stress of what was happening. . . . Well, my reaction to the stress was, of course, put it off. I managed to make it to one o'clock last night marking. I spent half the night looking over the house for the camera but still, I didn't get [the marking] done. . . . So I came in today very anxious and feeling very negative, almost to the point of depression, to find . . . [that you didn't] have the slides. I mean, there is no reason why I should have expected you to have the slides. It is part of the stress.*

Oliver introduced the problem of the three disruptive students (Steve, Jim, and John). The following excerpts indicate Taylor's view of some of the complexities and difficulties of working with these students:

157 **T**   *You see, John is German. David keeps calling him Hitler. They blew his cool today. John explained that to me after. It is interesting because he had the self-control to subdue himself and say, "Yes sir, OK sir," when I got mad at him. He didn't turn it, as many people have done and John has done — he has been in trouble with the office before because what he will do is turn it into a confrontation with the teacher. The anger level keeps going up and, if a teacher tries to get him to stop, he will turn around — you have seen this happen in general classes and in all kinds of classes. The anger is initially against a student. The teacher intervenes and the anger is directed towards the teacher.*

158 **O**   *Well, you were pretty heavy with him. I mean, there was no . . .*

159 **T**   *Did you see what he was doing? I only saw what John was doing, I never saw or heard what David did. He was kicking David really hard in the heel. . . . I thought the next thing is, David is going to punch him, and I have got a fight right in the middle of the microscopes, right in the middle of the class. So, I nailed him. . . .*

Later in the conference, on a more general note:

160 **T**   *There is lots of stuff going on in there but basically — we have talked about that already — it is a grade ten general class. There are a lot of dynamics in there. There are students in there that don't like each other and are not able to put those differences aside. There are kids in there that want attention. There are kids in there that are ready for the weekend, you know. . . .*

Within the context of weighing the pros and cons of kicking students out of class, Taylor pondered whether he was paying too big a price for his "soft discipline." Oliver related the discussion to context and continuity.

161 **O**   *You have one instance with that girl who showed up only one day this past week. The office has had her out [of school] and the family is supposed to get back in touch with us. She was tuned right out, the day she was here. So, you are willing to keep them in and pay a price there because in the long run it means less aggravation in terms of having to bring them up to scratch. . . . That is a point.*

162 **T**   *So much the way I operate depends on my relationship on an individual basis. If you give up on a kid by kicking her or him out for the day, you have lost that ability to have that personal interaction with the kid.*

Oliver tried to link some of the behaviour issues to context and continuity as it related to Taylor's diagrams on the board, as seen in the following:

163 **O**   *A couple of quickies. I have noticed a trend in terms of the kinds of things that you do on the board which I want to talk a little bit about. Where there are key events, you always go to the board and you always detail them for the kids and I think that is great. I like the idea that you were putting the date up and those kinds of general housekeeping things which are organizers for the kids. You tell them, OK, now I want you to take notes. All good organizational strategy. It's pedagogy that you are using to organize the kids. Yesterday, when we were talking about the [pap test], you went up and you did a nice diagram on the board, labelled vagina, cervix, etc., etc., clean and clear. The kids attended to that. They got the message. I also have noticed when you are at the board as well, like today for instance, you went up and you drew a cover slip, and a specimen and an air bubble and those kinds of things, and the field of view . . . and I have been trying to look at that a little bit, [from the point of view of continuity for a student]. I think what would be useful to the kids, based on the way I saw them react yesterday, would be to provide them with labels to that, just so that you can say nice and cleanly and clearly, "This is what this is." Jim may be turning around at the time you say, "This is a cover slip," and then comes back around and looks at the classroom and says, "Now, what is that," to himself. He may or may not. It is just a suggestion. Take it for what it is worth. It may be useful, it may not.*

164 **T**   *Good point.*

Generally, Oliver noted those points at which Taylor tied various issues together and linked students' work to things they had done in the past. The conference ended with more co-operative planning (O: "That is a nice sequence; so Monday is going to be mitosis"), and an offer of help by Oliver:

165 **O**   *OK, anything I can do for you, in terms of getting stuff together?*

166 **T**   *I think we are solidly underway here. I think I am fine. I think I will be fine for next week. The hospital trip is the only thing that I think is going to be too open ended. . . .*

167 **O**   *It is the context and continuity issue here. So often people go to the hospital, and it is an isolated incident. . . . But here it is tied directly to a program.*

168 **T**   *Yeah, and the only thing now is, you see, you saw the way I laid it out on the board for the kids. It is going to be difficult to work up, say, a question sheet, because the kids aren't even going to go to the same thing. . . . So, if you can offer me any kind of help at all, it would be to think about how we can organize these kids so that they have some structure to their day, [so they are] not just crowding around. . . .*

169 **O**   *Leave that to me.*

Considerations

The tone of this conference seemed different from those immediately preceding it. Although Oliver still assumed control of the conference by introducing issues and, especially, by giving praise for things done well, his tone was more accepting and clarifying than in some of the previous conferences. Aside from the praise given to Taylor and the general back-and-forth discussion (which I have not attempted to capture in the above conference) the following phrases indicate the tone:

170 **O**   *It is just a suggestion. . . .*
Take it for what it is worth. . . .
It may be useful, it may not. . . .
That is just another reflection. . . .
Your objective, as I read you. . . .
Is that fair [to say]? . . .

The point about the tone was corroborated in an interview between Taylor and myself later that day. An excerpt from that interview highlights why the issue of tone is important, especially with respect to the history of their relationship:

171 **T**   *I have been in a mentor-pupil relationship with Oliver for a long time because I started in the department as a very young teacher and he immediately adopted that sort of role. . . . I was afraid that that would be [continued in these conferences]. He is making very concerted efforts not to [act that way]. He always prefaces things: "I throw this out for your consideration." In the past, some of the problems that we have had is when I didn't want the mentor-student relationship any more. . . . Obviously, I also have had to work on our relationship so that we can function in a mutually profitable way, but that is the big thing for Oliver: "I throw this out for your consideration; don't get defensive; I want to know what your responses are; have you thought about this, that is all." He says those kinds of things when he is talking about the lesson. . . . When he prefaces it that way and leaves it as an intellectual discussion then it is not threatening and the feedback is positive. I can deal with it.*

Much later I had an interview with Oliver about an initial draft of the entire case on which I had asked him to comment. During our talk he kept coming back to this statement (171), and indicated that it was important for him to keep it in mind in his future work with his staff. It was clear that Taylor's statement had considerable impact on him and helped him see the way in which his approach could affect the feedback process. My view was that this was one of the few times that Oliver had received fairly direct commentary from a teacher. The impact of the comments highlighted the significance of an observer getting direct input from a teacher about feedback. As indicated earlier in this case, it is important that there is the possibility of open talk about the feedback process itself. The ability of the teacher and observer to do that skilfully is a learned art, but one that I believe is sorely needed if teachers are to work toward constructive relationships with each other in the feedback process.

Monday, Day 8

Returning to a Former Mode of Feedback

Taylor is pleased with his "chalk-talk" approach to the lesson, but Oliver is concerned. Oliver reverts to an earlier mode of feedback, raising a number of issues but neglecting to refer to context and continuity at critical points in the conference.

Class

This lesson consisted of a quiz, followed by an introduction to cell division. The quiz was made up of three questions. "List two differences between normal and cancerous cells. What is a pap test? Which type of biopsy did you perform last week?" The ensuing discussion constituted a brief review of aspects of previous work as is evident in the following excerpt:

172 **T**   *Now, cancerous cells divide quickly, they continue to divide, normal cells don't. Cancerous cells, because they divide so rapidly, are younger, OK? You will notice in the pap test slides we showed you, they stain differently if they are young or old. Second question. Biopsy. What do you look at the cells for?*

173 **S**   *To see if they are cancerous.*

174 **T**   *Right, Steve. The only way that you can tell absolutely positively whether cells are cancerous is to look at cells under the microscope. . . . That is what a pap test is. It is a biopsy of the, where?*

175 **S**   *Cervix.*

176 **T**   *I drew a diagram on the board for you of the uterus and the cervix and the vagina. The cervix is the neck of the womb. . . . Which biopsy did you do last week? . . .*

In the remainder of the class Taylor addressed the process of cell growth and division in normal cells as a prelude to a deeper understanding of the differences between normal and cancerous cells. Excerpts from his relatively lengthy talk have been selected to illustrate the technical complexity of the topic and the restlessness of some students:

177 **T** *At some microscopic size, the cell can no longer supply enough material, nor can it eliminate enough wastes to grow, and that is the limit to a cell. So, the question becomes, how do you add material when you reach this size? How do you add more cytoplasm? Nature seems to have solved this problem. Tim, how has nature solved this problem? You want to add more cytoplasm, you want this living creature to get bigger but it can't get bigger because of this limitation that I talk about. So, how does the cell solve the problem?*

178 **S** *It will reproduce. . . .*

179 **T** *Ah hah, good. . . . Now, understand what I am saying here. I will say it again. Cell division allows nature, shall we say, to increase the amount of living material where the cells themselves can't get any bigger. . . . Cell division is a major feature of both normal and cancerous cells, and it is also a means for telling them apart. We are not going to talk about all kinds of things that have to do with cells. What I want to consider is only the events in the nucleus, OK? The nucleus is the structure surrounded by a membrane inside. You were looking at your cheek cells on Friday. You saw the nucleus in the 35mm slides — it has a membrane around it, inside the cell. That is why it is stained so specifically separate from the rest — Steve! — why the nucleus stains differently from the rest. It is distinct because it has got a membrane around it to keep the nuclear stuff separate from the cytoplasm.*

[Later] Let's try and get through this. . . . You notice what is significant in the third diagram is that they have lined up in the middle and they are all attached to that centriole, the fibres. That third phase is called meta, middle, metaphase. The next one is anaphase. . . . Now, the centriole is like an anchor point, like a post, so the effect is to reel in the chromosomes and they are being pulled through the cytoplasm over to opposite ends of the cell — Steve! Take a look at this, Steve — all the information for a cell is on one side and all the information for a cell is on the other side. . . . Now take a look at the diagram once more and go quickly through it. OK, let's look at this again. The first diagram is called interphase. . . . In anaphase, those fibres contract, condense, get shorter, and since the centriole is like an anchor point it doesn't move. The chromosomes are the things that move. Now, they have got that shape, that V shape because of the drag created. So, for instance, if I were to make this a chromosome. There is one chromosome, here is another chromosome. What I am saying — Ralph! — What I am saying is, this is one complete set of genetic information for the hunk of DNA. It makes a second copy, and we will talk about that process tomorrow. . . .

Conference

Taylor began by talking about his teaching style:

180 **T**   *It felt fresh. I did something that I haven't done at all in this unit. I don't think I have. I have quizzed them before, but I don't think I have chalk-talked, which is the backbone of my teaching strength, I think. It was about time. The kids were getting a little fatigued, partly because I haven't been doing it very much. I try to get away with it in this course — get away from it in this course — because I don't think it is suited to them day after day. But, it is my strongest form of teaching. It is the one I am most comfortable in.*

181 **O**   *And how did you feel?*

182 **T**   *Fine, incredibly rambunctious. All the things that go through my mind while I teach. You know, I am teaching them the lesson, I am watching the dynamics in the room, I am looking at the flow of where I am going with the stuff I am talking about, I am thinking of which words to put on the board. I am also thinking of the personality of — the whole thing is all at once. The nice thing about this project is [that] . . . it doesn't just go. You [normally] go to your next class and forget it, it all dissolves and it is gone. . . . On top of all those other things, wow, it is amazing how much is going on in this room. They are perfectly prepared to work, but if they are not working, they are up the walls, because as soon as we got started, did you notice how quiet it got when that quiz started. . . .*

183 **O**   *You are also providing, the way I see it, continuity with the previous work by bringing them back to what we have learned before and [showing] how it relates to what we are doing today. . . .*

184 **T**   *There was the weekend between [so emphasizing continuity is more important] than, say, tomorrow or the next day.*

The conversation turned to the dynamics among key students. Taylor related the level of interplay in the classroom to management issues:

185 **T**   *[Ralph] is sucked in by Steve. Steve tends to be a bit of a model for them. Better student certainly. . . . I don't know, do you want to talk about classroom management, I don't know if that is the issue here?*

186 **O**   *I thought you handled the class very well. I mean, you allowed a certain amount of relaxation, yet you were committed to the sequence of events in the lesson and when it was necessary to push kids to attend, you did. There is a certain amount of exchange and interplay which keeps them satisfied, in that they are active, since in a lesson like this where you don't have any hands on things for them to do, they may need that.*

187 **T**   *It is really counter-productive to put the slammer on them and say, you know, the next person who talks is in trouble or something like that . . . because they can subvert anything. I don't mean to sound like I give up before I start because I don't think it is that negative of a thing. I am also just not that kind of person. If I were to start out that way, I would end up being incon-*

sistent because I could never maintain it in terms of my philosophy or my commitment. I think I am better [off being] a little more easy going on a consistent basis than to be inconsistent about when I don't want to kid, and when I do. You have to watch that, it is very much like with [my child], I have to watch it. Sometimes I am very tolerant of his horsing around and other times I get really mad at him. It depends on my moods. You have to be very careful with consistency, because the kid has no idea that this is one of the times when you have drawn the line and ten minutes ago you weren't drawing the line and, you know, they get upset with you when you are inconsistent. The same with the class. They are exactly the same. They get upset when you are inconsistent too. They will actively subvert whatever they feel is inconsistent. . . . Having gone this far, two or three months into the course, and having allowed a certain degree of freedom, a certain degree of chat . . . I don't think I can withdraw back and say, OK, now you have done it, everybody has to be quiet for the rest of the period, because that is inconsistent. It has nothing to do with the way I have taught them my expectations. I don't want them to go past [my expectations] in their testing. That is why I slam them so often now. You may notice that I am doing that [because] I don't want them to take it any further.

In the context of management, Oliver noted that students copied each other's answers during the quiz while Taylor's back was turned. Taylor was not concerned about this because, as he explained it, the function of the quiz was to review:

188   **T**   *I think [the quiz] was really the fastest way to zero in their attention. Honestly, and also, there were a few kids away today, and you get zero for a missed quiz. . . . That is fine with me. . . . And at a point when I want to monitor individuals, I move them further apart and I walk up and down the aisles. I look at everybody interact with everybody while they are working, and it is very easy for me to monitor. . . .*

The point about the quizzes turned out to be the first among several points that Oliver raised in fairly rapid succession as can be gleaned from the following excerpts:

189   **O**   *The other thing that I was thinking about as you were teaching, [to help] the guy who had trouble with the six sided cube on the blackboard, [you could] just provide them with hands-on things.*

190   **T**   *I remember, I just didn't feel like ducking out of the room.*

191   **O**   *No problem. . . . OK, the other thing is that, it would be nice if you could do, you know, the gelatin one where you place, maybe, potassium permanganate dye in gelatin and it diffuses. It would be nice to give them a demonstration if you could — I have forgotten, you know the one I am talking about.*

192   **T**   *Just in order to show how far the stuff will go.*

Taylor explained why he did not do the demonstration commonly used to illustrate the issue, and instead chose to show it on the blackboard. This brought up the issue of labelling diagrams which had been a recurrent concern for Oliver. In his response, Taylor made an important distinction:

193 **O**   *I thought this hung together very nicely. You did a good job on the board of depicting it. The diagrams were good. Steve still gives you the odd shot but one of the things which you notice, which you did now, is you are labelling your diagrams. . . . For me that was great. I saw that as a plus.*

194 **T**   *You mean this sheet, this handout?*

195 **O**   *Well, yeah, all the diagrams that you did today on the board, you labelled.*

196 **T**   *I think the difference was not so much that I responded to you. I don't think I responded to you, but I think I did a different type of lesson from the one that you noticed. In that other lesson I think what I did was try to organize myself with the diagram while I was explaining to them. Sometimes you reach for words. . . . What I am saying is I don't think I improved my teaching since our conversation. I think what I have done is I have taught a different style of lesson where, "This is stuff for your notebooks," and it is part of an organized lesson. The other was an off-the-cuff response to a question to an individual kid.*

197 **O**   *Yeah, I see the distinction.*

198 **T**   *So, you were right, it should have been labelled, it should have been there. As you say, Jim turned around and missed it, you know, and turned back. But, I just admit this in all fairness, I didn't learn from what you said.*

199 **O**   *That is fine. Can I bring a couple of things up here? That was a really nice issue that Tom brought out about the brain cells.*

Oliver continued with the observation that Tom seemed very bright and that it might be interesting to push him a bit more in class.

200 **T**   *There is the limitation, working with these kids. If you flush something out with Tom, and the other guys are punching each other in the back corner, it is a big limitation.*

The bulk of the remainder of the conference concerned what could be done to provide students with evidence, particularly with regard to the claim that all living things are made of cells.

201 **O**   *But there is evidence that one could bring to bear on that which would substantiate, you know — the point is, you don't have the evidence for them at this point and this is based on your knowledge and other people's knowledge, just as when you. . . .*

202 **T**   *Right, or empirically, it is based on reasoning it out first and going to the lab and saying, "Now, what experiments can we set up to test this."*

203 **O**   *Yeah, that is nice. . . .*

     [Later] *What is of interest to me, and this is not only a consequence of the lesson, but I am sitting there and I am trying to think where that kid is, and [I'm] saying, "What in his experience" — and I am not just talking about your class or anything like that — "What in his experience leads him to the understanding or the ability to accept a statement like that?" What do they get in grade nine? What do they see on the TV? How do they know? It is the whole issue of knowing. . . . Yeah, I agree with you. The issue for me is a wider thing. It set me off because if I look back at these kids. Let's say David [taught them] in grade nine, and when he hit the cell unit, he said, "This is a cell and there are lots of cells in the human body. I am going to show a plant cell." OK, and we might look at, I don't know, let's put a prepared plant cell underneath. So they may or may not see a whole number of cells. And [suppose] in grade seven and eight they are given a class like this and maybe they see, hear something on the news, as Tom did today. Deep down inside I am saying to myself, "What real kinds of tangible evidence do kids have that organisms, large and small, are made up of cells." I mean you and I would look under microscopes a lot. We see them. We see films and it is not a big deal.*

204 **T**   *If it is a big deal, you deal with it . . . because we have the mechanism right here. Look at all these slides here. You could say, "I would like you to look through these. I have picked representative plants, animals, fungi, monerans, protists. I want you to look at all these things. I want you to notice that all of these things are made up of these same compartments that we call cells."*

205 **O**   *I don't disagree, but . . .*

206 **T**   [Interjects] *But, you see, the relative importance — again context and continuity — you are going off on a whole evidence side issue. So you are right and your [point is] valid. Everything you are saying is interesting, but I think [evidence] is second to the overriding concerns of teaching the stuff. . . . What will happen is, two years from now in grade eleven biology, all of a sudden you think that [evidence] is neat to push on the kids, and it becomes your thrust. . . .*

207 **O**   *You know, the issue for me is knowing what the kids have in their bag of evidence, that is the key.*

208 **T**   *[You mean] how well they have been taught to be critical about the information that is thrown at them. I think they are very selective about it, just as we are selective in the things that we back up and want them to understand. . . . This [issue about cell division] is one that I just threw at them. Other things I have really looked at very carefully and said well, you have*

no direct evidence for this. . . . How would you investigate this? We select because we don't want that to be the middle lesson all the time. . . .

209 **O** *I wasn't being critical of that one. The thing that I was thinking about was your comment a while back, [suggesting that] we have got to get our act together and see what we are doing in grade ten and grade eleven, grade twelve and grade thirteen. That just hit me, and I was thinking, yeah, you are absolutely right because we make certain assumptions — and we are doing this all the time — that they have this piece of evidence or that they have got this background.*

Considerations

The discussion concerning evidence began a consideration of the impact of cumulative learning in science as students move through the entire system. The discussion also provoked Taylor's questions concerning the relationships between espoused curriculum beliefs like "critical thinking" (e.g., 208, "How well they have been taught to be critical about the information that is thrown at them"), and the laundry list of knowledge students are expected to acquire (206, "Everything you are saying is interesting, but I think [evidence] is second to the overriding concerns of teaching the stuff").

Although there is abundant evidence in the transcript of the conference that Oliver was supportive of and felt positive about Taylor's lesson, Oliver's comments add up to an insurmountable list of things that could be attended to. In this respect the conference had a tone similar to that of Day 2 — on both occasions numerous issues were addressed. The following statement exemplifies this as well as other points which I shall briefly outline:

210 **O** *OK, another thing that hit me, and again it's a small issue, but I think when you are adding up, summating, the small issues leading to confusion in, you know, the general student — when you went through and explained and used that diagram as an organizer, I thought that was really good. It was clear. The students could attend. You put it on the board. You personalized it, and you went through and labelled it. You talked and pushed on some of the things that they might not have remembered, defined terms for them, and you defined chromosome. . . . But what didn't happen — the relationship between DNA and the chromosome was not alluded to.*

Oliver's comment about "adding up . . . the small issues" (210) appropriately assumed that confusion for a student can be an accumulative process. But, in terms of the feedback process, such a comment might be regarded as nitpicking, especially if the teacher has demonstrated considerable effort with respect to context and continuity. An observer could address the issue by dropping small points altogether or by reiterating that they are "small points" by showing why.

The phrase, "but what didn't happen" (210), highlights a real tension in the process: to what extent should the discussion dwell on what has passed as opposed to what might be done in the future? Both focusses are necessary, but emphasis on what has passed can easily be interpreted by the teacher as disapproval. Future-referenced comments at least concern events over which the teacher can exercise some control.

It turned out that Taylor *had* made a connection between DNA and chromosomes, but Oliver missed it. Such a slip affects the credibility of the feedback process, and increases the risk of focussing the discussion on the veracity of the data rather than on an analysis of what the data (variously constructed) could mean. (For example, if Oliver missed the connection, it might be that some of the students missed it as well.)

The process is meant to be collegial, involving two peers who conduct an analysis of teaching events, but Oliver takes the prerogative of commenting (positively or negatively) about Taylor's teaching. This in itself seems to imply an uneven power base which can produce concerns about trust and skepticism about the process. A didactic demeanor can also contribute to a tone incompatible with collegiality. For instance, this Monday's conference was less characterized by qualifiers ("I offer this for your consideration") than the conference on the previous Friday. In a later interview Oliver said that conferences seemed less didactic when he had been working alongside Taylor during the labs. On those occasions he discussed issues with the students and with Taylor and there tended to be a natural carry over from those discussions into the conference.

Also contributing to tension in the process is the possibility that Taylor did not see the connection between "evidence" and issues of reasons, context, and continuity (206). Oliver did not make the connection explicit. When these connections remain implicit, the teacher may question how they pertain to central issues. At the heart of such concerns lie questions about the boundaries of the discussion. In this project there was explicit agreement about feedback on issues of reasons, context, and continuity, but obviously any given issue of teaching lies on a continuum of relevance to those central concerns. The more an issue is perceived as peripheral to the central concern, the more important it is for the observer to make the connections explicit; a perceived transgression of implicit or explicit boundaries can draw the process itself into question.

Finally, Taylor's point, when he suggested that the issue of evidence might at some time in the future become a "thrust" (206), should be considered carefully. He may envision addressing the point about evidence more extensively than Oliver intended. With respect to cell theory, for example, it might have been sufficient for Taylor to simply say something like: "Our work will assume one of the major theories in biology — the idea that all living material is made of cells — although we will not retrace the thinking and observations that led to such a theory." Grounding Taylor and Oliver's conference discussions in concrete examples could help avoid divergent interpretations of issues raised — a divergence which can have a detrimental effect on the process.

On this Monday, Taylor obviously felt positive about the "chalk-talk" lesson. His comments suggest that some of his enthusiasm resulted from his ability to control the class while he monitored what he was saying with regard to continuity and meaning. (Control was more problematic for Taylor, as with many teachers, during extended laboratory situations.) If my characterization of the tone of the conference is accurate, Oliver may have felt freer to push on issues this Monday because he felt his relationship with Taylor was stronger and could stand more stress. He and Taylor had worked hard on the substance, process, and interpersonal aspects of their work together the previous Thursday, and as a result had ended their conference on Friday on a high note. Oliver might also have been following the rule of thumb that the time to push hard is when a teacher is strongest and most resilient. As with most rules of thumb there is a grain of practical truth to the notion, but an observer must also be careful not to underestimate the need to attend to nuances of the process (qualifiers, continued reference to the central focus of the interaction, number of issues being discussed, etc.) and not to overestimate the teacher's resilience. Deciding when to push on issues is always a point of judgement for a participant-observer, one which has no easy solution.

Tuesday, Day 9

More Talk About the Process

Further aspects of the personal dimension of teaching emerge from talk about discipline and from Oliver's candid remarks about his own frustration. The episode is a reminder of how a few disruptive students add to a teacher's stress.

Class

Taylor began this lesson by using a deck of playing cards to demonstrate the role of DNA in cell division:

211 **T** *What I woud like to do right now is outline for you exactly what appears to go on in a cell when it duplicates its genetic material. OK, I want to go over mitosis again. We are going to use an organizer that I found, using flow charts and playing cards, and what I would like you to do initially is simply to watch while I try and explain the situation to you. . . . Now what I am going to do here is try and use playing cards to represent the genetic material. I am going to use the tape to stick them up to the board. I am going to go through the phases of mitosis, and try to get a couple of concepts across. . . .*

[Demonstration] *What is important for the growth is that the genetic material doubles, but notice, keep in mind, this is the same as that. This is the same as that. This is the same and this is the same, so these cells will be under the same control mechanisms. These cells will have the same characteristics. Daughter cells are identical to the parent cell. There is continuity from generation to generation. . . .*

The second part of the lesson consisted of a film on cell division. Taylor connected the point of the film to the previous demonstration and highlighted the complex phases of cell division as can be seen in these excerpts:

212 **T** *OK, now I have a film that is going to be our last run through this. It is a good film. It really portrays this [process of mitosis] visually quite well. I want you to keep an eye on this and we will talk about it as it runs.*

213 **Film** *Here is the process of mitosis in a living plant cell. In living plant cells the spindle is not apparent.*

214 **T**   *Notice that it doesn't go step by step. It is one flowing thing. Those phases have been artificially set up by people who have taken photographs, stop frame, and identified separate parts. It is a continuous process.*

215 **Film** *The process of mitosis is continuous but it is possible to identify four general phases, each characterized by specific activity.*

In the last part of the lesson Taylor went over several information sheets on cancer which related the differences between normal and cancerous cells to the process of cell division:

216 **T**   *This sheet is called "The Wild Cells." You will notice some of the objectives of the booklet if you look at the title of the first page, "What Is Cancer?" The two pages that follow are diagrams, one which shows you mitosis, which we have just done, mitosis in animal cells, and the next one which is abnormal cell division, OK? So I want to look at all three of those sheets at the same time. . . . I want you to take a look with me at the three pages. First of all the reading, all the dark print, the middle of the second column — mitosis in animal cells, figure one and figure two, abnormal cell division, O.K? [Taylor reads:] "Normal and abnormal cell division in cancer. One of the most striking aspects of tumor cells is their tendency to divide abnormally. These abnormal divisions result in very unusual cells. Some very large, some small, but with huge nuclei. . . ."*

Conference

Several issues were worth attending to in this conference given Oliver and Taylor's discussions thus far. The first concerned Steve, who had once again been disruptive during the class. Taylor took the lead:

217 **T**   *OK, I made a list of things I wanted to make sure that I wouldn't forget. Soon we will be done and I will never have said anything. . . . I wrote down a whole bunch of overall concerns that I wanted to talk about but let's talk about the lesson quickly first. I don't know where to start, but I think Steve has got to come up sooner or later, and Jim — I think classroom management is now becoming a problem with regard to those guys. . . .*

218 **O**   *Do you want to analyze a little bit and suggest some strategies? Do you want to deal with any of the issues or do you want to identify. . . .*

219 **T**   *I talked to them at the end. They were not that keen to listen to me and they had an audience and so on, but I think probably what I am going to do is have a little talk with Steve tomorrow before class starts. Out of class, one-to-one, just off on the side and make it clear to him that this isn't acceptable. He sure was a lot more attentive when I told him if Jim went he went. They were egging each other on. . . .*

220 **O**   *And don't forget that coupled in with that issue of management is the thing*

that you alluded to, the issue of insults in the classroom. I mean he is obviously insulting you and you might push on it that way. If one looks at the transcripts and looks at what you said to Steve today, I think you will find it revealing. Maybe not.

221 **T**   *It was an insult. It was just funny in that it is not the way I normally talk. . . .*

222 **O**   [Interjects] *No, I am not only looking at that issue, but the number. . . .*

223 **T**   *Oh, the flak back and forth, yeah. Oh I know, it was in my mind while we were doing it. I couldn't get over it. It was really bugging me. I thought to myself, at what point — you see, if anything, what I have to do is I have to sit back and wonder to what extent am I being too lenient. Probably if I really do stop and reflect on it very much I am going to realize that I shouldn't be allowing Steve to remain and do those things. And probably, in the long run, it would be better for him to have the repercussions and all the things that go with it, all the negative things in terms of him learning science and his attitude towards me. But I think his attitude has deteriorated to the point where it is not a productive one anyway. So he gets mad at me because I slam him. . . .*

A second issue raised in the conference concerned how the unit needed to be changed. Within that discussion, Oliver praised Taylor for the lesson in terms of the intellectual connections made for the students. Out of this praise grew Oliver's admission of his own sense of frustration. This gave Taylor a chance to talk further about the professional context within which a teacher works:

224 **O**   *I felt, as a supervisor, that you were much better prepared than you had been in the past.*

225 **T**   *Didn't I tell you before class that I was really on a roll today. And, you know, I did sit down and I worked on it.*

226 **O**   *Yeah, you told me last night that you had done all the marking which made you feel good. You didn't tell me that you had worked through the unit. I think — I will be quite honest, you felt my frustration in the past, you know, the last two or three lessons when you have been on a downer and have been frustrated yourself. I have been frustrated too because I haven't seen — you do, I know, what you can do because of these conditions.*

227 **T**   *Which is the real world. Teachers go in cycles and I went through a tired low cycle and I am on a high now. It just kicked in. Yesterday was OK. Today was better. Yeah, really clicking. And tomorrow is going to be fine because I am on a roll — but part of the business of teaching is the fact that, unlike other types of endeavours where standards can be maintained despite personal highs and lows, you are in there by yourself. If you have a headache the class runs very differently, no matter how much material you have got prepared. . . . Heck, maybe if you had to pee and didn't get there before class*

starts, it can change the whole outcome of the class, or an interaction. It is so personal and emotional and based on the personality of the teacher.

Considerations

One of the recurring concerns in this case study is the stress experienced by a teaccher. That stress comes from within the professional setting of teaching and from outside that setting, in the teacher's personal life. The beginning of the Day 9 conference between Taylor and Oliver is an explicit reminder that classroom control can be a constant threat to a teacher's peace of mind. Two or three disruptive students are all that are needed to make issues of control a preoccupation for a teacher. Taylor is not preoccupied with control, but it is clear that he finds the behaviour of Steve and his friends upsetting and problematic. Taylor, like most teachers, wants to be liked by his students. He places a high premium on the interpersonal aspects of his work with students, interacting with them freely and easily on a one-to-one basis outside the formalities of day-to-day lessons. His comments at the beginning of the conference suggest that he is grappling with the difficult question of how to deal adequately with control without alienating students and giving up the interpersonal aspect of his work.

Personal pressures outside the professional setting have also affected how Taylor has been able to respond to the demands of teaching, and have affected the nature of his work with Oliver. This was frustrating for Oliver, but today's conference was the first occasion in which he verbally expressed that frustration (226). In a later interview Taylor pointed out that, had Oliver expressed frustration when he (Taylor) was depressed, he would have found it very threatening. As it was, Taylor felt that Oliver was speaking honestly and the fact that Oliver talked about his own feelings (some of which were expressed off the record) helped to build trust. According to Taylor, "It is very positive to hear this because . . . it makes me have more confidence in [Oliver] because he can bury the stuff that would lead to confrontation — [and] talk about it later as a positive aspect of the process."

Wednesday, Day 10
Boundaries of Discussion

> Oliver addresses the issue of the individual student projects, an aspect of the lesson he did not comment on the preceding week (Day 5). The nature of his comments introduces a question about the boundaries of discussion.

Class

As usual for a Wednesday, the first half hour of the class was devoted to student projects. Four students did demonstrations which, although unrelated to each other and to the cancer unit, were interesting and held the attention of the class, save the usual inattentive group who spent the time talking. Following the presentations, Taylor gave a quiz, separating students he caught copying. In the ten minutes which remained after the quiz, he addressed continuity by forecasting what they would be doing on the following day:

228 **T** *OK — Doug, Steve — what we are going to do now is, we are going to move into the specific cancer that I want to deal with, as an example, and that is lung cancer. Tomorrow we are going to take a look at normal lung structure and function because, as I have written down here, in order to understand the cancer situation you have to understand what the normal functioning of the lung is, how it functions, so that we can understand what cancer does and [how it] interrupts that [normal functioning] and kills a person. . . . What is it about lungs that makes it such a fatal type of cancer? What is it about human beings that causes them to get lung cancer? Now one of the things that we are going to have to do also is to look at this concept of differentiation. I haven't written the definition down here because I wanted you to listen — Steve, put your computer stuff away and get your notebook out — differentiation is the process by which a cell, which has no special function, becomes specialized as a lung cell or a brain cell or a nerve cell or a stomach cell. . . . OK, now, tomorrow we are going to work through some very simple material that will help us understand normal lungs and then I want to look at overheads. We talked about those the first day when I started [this unit]. . . . I want to look at photographs of normal lungs, and photographs of cancerous lungs. On the trip to the hospital you will get a chance to look at them for real. . . . We are going to look at them under the*

microscope tomorrow. We have got a number of things to do tomorrow. And of course the last thing I am interested in looking at is what is the cause of lung cancer. I have a few newspaper articles and a few statistics to look at.

Conference

Taylor opened the discussion with concerns about discipline during the student presentations and his particular concern about one potentially violent student:

229 **T**   *It is something that is very difficult to deal with but did you notice how he disintegrated as that project went on? Almost to the point where I would call it clinical. And one wonders how to deal with that as a classroom teacher. I think to myself, "I can't handle that for five more weeks." I am certainly not going to start anything like, "Your kid has a mental disorder, or is disturbed or has learning disabilities." It is funny how the pressure is on a teacher, and that becomes a monumental task to decide to take the plunge and do something about a kid. . . . But a very difficult situation there. It is their project and yet they are really undisciplined.*

Oliver tried to link the nature of the student projects to the issue of discipline, but the weight of his comment fell on questioning the value of the projects. He questioned the role of the projects in terms of what the students might be learning about science, rather than explicitly in terms of the unit and issues of context and continuity. Taylor responded with a lengthy justification for the activities. Oliver pressed on the usefulness of having students mark each other's presentations: "The question that I want to ask is, what kinds of criteria do you give students here for evaluating other students?" The discussion around this point, and around the projects in general, consumed a substantial portion of the conference.

The conference then turned to the quiz and Oliver focussed on the manner in which Taylor separated students so they could not copy. Two different views emerged:

230 **O**   *You [could] say, OK, now it is test time so spread out. Interesting the way you do it, and I am not making a value judgement. I am just pointing out things of interest. The way you do it, it means that you have to be the police officer. In other words, your role becomes that of being the observer and watching the situation and then identifying what you construe to be evidence for them, incriminating information. That requires you to watch around the classroom and make those judgements.*

231 **T**   *It also gives the students the message that I work on the basis of trust and I work on the basis of status quo. You sit here, [unless] I get evidence to the contrary. So on the one hand, yes, I am a police officer. On the other hand I feel that I am trying to give them a message there which is, "I trust you, we will go from there."*

232 **O**   *Fine, that is your way of doing things. . . .*

Considerations

An issue emerging from this conference concerns the question of what topics are out-of-bounds for discussion. If Oliver decides to introduce the issue of the student projects, the only legitimate grounds for doing so would be that they break the continuity of the unit on cancer and cell biology. That link between his observation and the focus of feedback in this case study (context and continuity) would have to be made explicit. But even though raising the issue might be warranted, it is not at all clear that it would be a wise thing to do since the projects are part of Taylor's established weekly routine.

Generally speaking, feedback needs to be related to the agreed upon focus. The reasoning behind this arises from a conception of feedback as collegial, genuinely helpful to the teacher (but not reduced to vacuous praise), and as that which keeps the interests of the students firmly in mind. What constitutes "real collegiality" is problematic, of course, and is one of the implicit issues which runs through this case. One way to establish collegiality is to ensure that the teacher has, and is seen to have, considerable control over what will be discussed in a feedback conference. Further, if there has been a mutually agreed upon focus for feedback (as in this case), then the feedback must be (and must be seen to be) related to that focus. Otherwise the process tends to revert to an "old style supervision," where the observer assumes the right to zero in on anything she or he regards as important.

This does not mean that there is always a clear distinction between "in" and "out-of-bounds" discussion. For example, as working concepts, one of the liabilities of "context" and "continuity" is that they can be stretched to include most of what goes on in a classroom. But not everything worthy of thorough discussion in *some* context should be discussed. Having a focus provides the participants with a mutually understood reference point which can be returned to when the discussion begins to overrun the boundaries and to compromise the collegial intent of the process. In this respect, Oliver might have been pushing very hard those boundaries when he questioned Taylor's practice of peer-evaluation and the manner in which Taylor separated students during the quiz.

Thursday, Day 11

Constructive Feedback Deteriorates

> Taylor reflects on timing, a common difficulty with lab exercises. Oliver provides positive and constructive feedback about context and continuity, but the conference deteriorates over the microscopes.

Class

The first ten minutes of the lesson were spent going over Wednesday's quiz. The next activity involved the whole class looking at 35 mm projections of normal and cancerous cells of a variety of tissues (cervix, moles, lung). Taylor provided the most input by drawing attention to those features of the slides that were important to the lesson. When slides of lung tissue were shown, students became much more actively involved. This presented a dilemma for Taylor since he realized that time was short:

233 **S**   *Sir, you know when you smoke, right? The tar goes down into your lungs. If he stops smoking, would that go away?* [Students talking during this question.]

234 **T**   *It depends when — excuse me. I know everybody has got an opinion and everybody is interested in smoking and cancer, but I will talk.*

235 **S**   *We listen.*

236 **T**   *Thank you. If your cells develop to the point of what they call a pre-cancerous condition, you are getting close to the point at which you can't repair it. . . .*

237 **S**   *Are they finding cures for cancer?*

238 **T**   *Wednesday's lesson, Steve. I hate to cut you off like that, Wednesday's lesson.*

239 **S**   *How do they not know that it is something simple like, you know.*

240 **T**   *Remember what he is asking. When they are curing it or diagnosing it? Which word do you want to use? When they make a decision that it is cancer . . .*

241 **S**   [Interjects] *Yeah, when they know that it is cancer, what do they . . .*

242 **T**   [Interjects] *Wednesday's lesson, Steve. I will say right now, very quickly, they will surgically remove or they will put chemicals in your body that kill cancer cells or they will put radiation on the cells and kill them with radiation, OK. We will talk about that in detail.*

The final exercise involved looking at prepared slides of normal and cancerous kidney tissue, and drawing a diagram. In spite of Steve's protests ("Why does he give us fifteen minutes? . . . And then you wonder why we don't finish, eh?"), Taylor made it quite clear that they would continue the work on the following day. Here are excerpts from the final part of the lesson:

243 **T**   *I want to see if everybody can have a look at the kidney slides today. I will get the slides, the cupboard is open. If you have forgotten which microscope you were supposed to use, I have it written down. Brown's class, period one, had the microscopes out, so check carefully. He says he has checked them all. That means that they should be in perfect order, otherwise you may be blamed. Pencil? OK, there is work to be done. . . .*

When you go to high power, please remember to focus away from the slide so you don't run the high power lens through the slide. The kidney is a blood filtering organ so you will probably see blood vessels with blood cells inside. In the normal kidney, the ones that stain very dark are blood cells. . . .

A good point has come up. You can't pick out the things that should be drawn unless you look at both slides. It is probably a good idea to compare the two first and then think about what to draw to show the differences. Tom was having trouble figuring out what to draw on the first slide because you don't know what you are comparing it to. Look at both first. . . .

We will continue tomorrow and I will ask you to hand these in tomorrow after class, not today, so don't worry about finishing. I would like one person in the group to put the slides back and put them in the slide box and the other person to put the microscope away. Power off. Turn them onto low power. Brown is very concerned about them being under low power when you have finished. Wrap the cord around. Put the cover on and put it back in the proper space. I would love to get my pencils back. Thank you.

Conference

Taylor took the lead by expressing concern about the timing of the two parts of the lesson. As can be seen in the following, this led him to work out how the sequence could be adjusted in the future:

244 **T**   *It probably was the wrong place to do those 35 mm slides. Up until I pulled them out and looked at them, I was convinced that this was a good time to do them. That is just one of those things that you find out and you change your mind about. Had we done a pre-class before we started I would have said, I want to do these 35 mm slides right here and the overheads and get*

going on lung cancer. You know, that is the way it goes. I looked at myself and I thought, why am I not doing this next week? . . .

245 **O**   *How did you arrive at that sequence that you went through?*

246 **T**   *Ah, initially I didn't have any lung cancer slides so I wasn't sure if I was going to do any more microscopy. I thought we had lung cancer and I talked to [another teacher] and they were all tuberculosis. So it was just a misunderstanding. So all of a sudden I thought, well, if we are not going to do it now, we will look at the rest of the anatomy. Then I thought about it some more. And I thought if we have got the normal kidney and the cancerous kidney, and the normal liver and the cancerous liver, why not stick with cancer. . . .*

[Later in the discussion] *I have got to the point where I have prepared too much and, for the lesson to be the way I wanted it, it should have started and ended with the material that I wanted to cover. . . .*

247 **O**   *Where would you end it?*

248 **T**   *I think I would do the microscopy all in one class but the other stuff isn't a full period's worth of work. I think what one should have done was microscopy all day today, and then tomorrow, slides and overheads, and into a discussion of causes of cancer.*

249 **O**   *I don't know whether I agree with you and the reason I say that is because at the beginning — the kids' attention to the slides in particular. Sure some are gross and you got those comments, but the fact that you have up there on the board some evidence of cancer and how it generally looks and you are able to show them the cancerous lung versus the normal lung; and you talked about the presence of carbon in the lungs. It was certainly a focal point. I think you gave them a good jumping off place to actually then look for evidence.*

250 **T**   *That is nice to hear because I was wondering whether that was too weak to justify. It is good to hear that from you because obviously that was the way I wanted to do it. I was wondering whether — in fact, you see, the thing that I walk away with is the feeling of disappointment. The thing that disappoints me is the fact that we started microscopy too late in the period. . . . [The pap smear overheads] really belong somewhere else. And probably with those [overheads] out and doing the 35 mm slides — and not taking up the test, which I never thought of. All I figured was, "I am going to mark tonight, tomorrow I am going to do the slides." I never thought, "It takes ten minutes to discuss the test." There is ten minutes out of the class, right? Not that it matters that much but between the two of them, there is twenty minutes. And there is the kidney drawing to be handed in. So really you see, maybe my lesson — now that we talk it out — maybe the lesson wasn't too long but at the last minute I shoved a couple of extra items in that I shouldn't have.*

. . . The pap test one should be way back when I drew that diagram on the side board, instead of [using] the overhead today, right? . . .

251 **O**   *Can you do me a favour? Tonight can you take your copy of this program and take five or ten minutes — or this afternoon, whenever you can find it — and make some notes as to where you think those particular resource materials should go so we don't lose them, and I will do the same because what I want to do is, I want to come back at the end when you and I have some time, and we will sit down and we will just make some suggestions about how we can change this unit.*

Oliver addressed the issues of context and continuity and pointed out that Taylor was more explicit than he had been previously with regard to what he wanted from students. In the discussion Taylor made an important point about the feedback project:

252 **O**   *I am trying to look over my notes. You reviewed the nature of the cancer cell. You gave them context.*

253 **T**   *I jumped around too much. I jumped around too much which encourages their jumping around.*

254 **O**   *OK, but there was an awful lot of tying back to the previous lessons so that when they attended to actually looking at the prepared slides — and notice; this time you were much more explicit and I was really happy to see that. I would say that one of the real strengths of this lesson is that you told them precisely what you wanted. . . . You see, what I am trying to push on in this interview is to look at things that I see as being consequences of you and I talking. . . . Let me push on one other thing. When you dealt with Steve and someone else. . . . First of all you started, you know, "pssst," to Steve. You bent forward, good behaviour basically [and said] "It is hard for me to concentrate when you are talking, so keep it down." He comes back again, "Sir, sir," and he tries to get you sidetracked and you say to him, "Steve, this is tomorrow's class," and he keeps persisting and you say, "Steve," you said it twice, "this is tomorrow's lesson," and so you maintain the integrity of his request. You say three things, "Removal, chemical, radiation and that is it, Steve." You don't get hooked. Because he tries to hook you all the time. I thought that was extremely good. There was an awful lot of teacher talk today, "What I want you to do is this and this."*

255 **T**   *Are you trying to make a point here?*

256 **O**   *Yeah I am. I am trying to make a point that you were much more directive today, OK?*

257 **T**   *That has a lot to do with the fact that — and I was yesterday, too — it has a lot to do with the fact that I am in here now. I am no longer tired from my previous commitments. It also took me a certain amount of time, you know. . . . I think it is important to understand that there is a settling down time.*

I found it took me a certain amount of time to be able to deal with the time it takes [to do the project] because you see the time it takes is out of my school day. I spend no time on this project outside of school. It is coming out of my down time and my spares and my preparation time. And it took me a while. . . . And I think now this has become routine for me, the fact that we are doing this study, and that makes a difference in my preparation for class because now I have worked out where and when to prepare for class when all this time is taken up. . . .

The last few comments made by Taylor were a reminder that it takes time to re-establish a daily routine and rhythm when an unusual circumstance is introduced. Oliver then set the context for dealing with several other issues:

258 **O**   *What I would really like to push on a little more today is the process, if we could, because there are a number of things that I have been, not keeping back, but haven't had a chance to attend to. I sat down last night and did an awful lot of thinking, and some reading, and tried to prepare some things that I wanted to share with you so that you could deal with them if you wanted to. Tell me I am full of crap if you want to. And, we can play around with it. I think the issues of context and continuity came through here really well today. I was so pleased with that. You know, you are constantly going back and reviewing new terms. You are dealing with sequencing, I thought it was good. . . .*

There were two main issues that Oliver spent time on. The first concerned those students in the class that Taylor interacted with less frequently than others; a second issue concerned the use of the microscopes:

259 **O**   *You have certain expectations for your students. They would be able to — by a certain point — handle the microscope for instance, and have all the requisite skills so that when you throw a lung slide at them, bang, they have got it. And, what I observe may be different from your expectations. What I am presenting to you are some observations. . . . Observations, OK. Today [with the microscope], my expectations for success were higher than what the kids achieved in two areas: number one, the ability to get a slide on high power very quickly and easily without any assistance from you or me. And, secondly, to put the microscopes away in such a manner that Brown would be happy if he came back next period, OK? My feeling was that they — and I am giving you straight goods now — my feeling was that they did not fulfill those expectations to the point that I would want to have them at this point in the sequence. How do you react to that?*

At this juncture Taylor reminded Oliver of the difficulty in teaching some students and how that related to the issue of expectations:

260 **T**   *They didn't meet my expectations for getting the [microscopes] out carefully. And I think that comes back to what a general profile is. The way these kids are behaving in a group situation in that class, their degree of responsibili-*

ty, their degree of responsiveness, their degree of co-operation and work and attention to detail is almost random from day to day. Today they are on, tomorrow they are not. From an individual point . . . I would never have expected that [David would hold a microscope over his head, slightly upside down], but that to me epitomizes a general student. If I were to lecture somebody on general students, I would love to have a videotape of that and say, "Look, here is this kid, he has done an excellent microscopy unit and look at him get the microscope out from the cupboard." That is a general student. I don't know where you want to go with this but I don't feel that's preparation and classroom management. I really don't think so. Now, that is debatable since I haven't made it so tough. . . .

Oliver continued to press the issue. Taylor's response indicated his frustration:

261 **O**   *I think that is something that you have to wrestle with. . . . I can offer you my perceptions but I don't think that is appropriate. I think that what you have to deal with at this point is the fact that the students are not meeting what I would expect, and what you would expect after this amount of time, and you have to reflect back on why and perhaps [try] some other strategies.*

262 **T**   *Well, I think alternatives have to be looked at to find out whether it is because . . . that is going to be one of the symptoms of the general student, or whether it was because of the [teaching] strategy. I understand what you are saying. The other thing that I think, as far as focussing under high power, it is remarkable how many kids didn't and this is what I expected. So, in fact my expectations weren't that high. I expected a lot of, "I don't know what to draw," you know, and that has a lot to do with the fact that they have no experience. They have had their microscopes out three times. That is no experience. That is not enough experience — but the handling of them, I expected to be better. . . . Obviously, at some point we have to talk about classroom expectations and techniques, because I know you are dying to tell me what is inappropriate. No, you know, what I am trying to say. We won't take that any further right now, but I really feel that there are very different opinions about some of my classroom strategies. This is the tip of the iceberg with these microscopes. Fair enough, and we should [look] at that constructively because, if all this is constructive, I am sure that would be too.*

263 **O**   *I welcome that, I really do.*

264 **T**   *Because I know you want to talk about some things, and it is fair and we will. Now, what I wanted to say, though, is I wonder if this rapid fire stuff, this busy stuff, this overprepared stuff sets me up. Like, I just cannot extend myself any further to watch all of the microscopes, because I have got this for them, that for them, and this for them and that for them, and "Oh, watch that microscope." I am doing too much at one time. And maybe some of my classroom organization needs to revolve around having a free hand at all times. Maybe, in order to have better management over some of these things, [I need] to have one hand empty at all times in class, which provides a dif-*

ferent strategy in terms of preparation and teaching. Not discipline, like, "You sit down and shut up," "You have a detention." None of that stuff. I couldn't change into that anyway. But I was getting the feeling, I thought to myself, my God, I am running around like a chicken with my head cut off today. . . .

Considerations

The first part of the conference (244-254) has a particularly positive tone, and is a fine example of constructive feedback. Oliver connnected the specifics of what happened in the classroom to the issues of context and continuity and the behaviour of the students. These connections were made with a view to future changes in the unit.

A less constructive tone developed toward the end of the conference. Taylor expressed his frustration clearly: he cannot be all things to all people. The context surrounding his frustration is important to recognize. Over the course of their work together, Taylor had attended, in one way or another, to nearly every item of feedback from Oliver, regardless of the tone of their conversation at the time. In the construction of this case I have not been able to include all of the pertinent instances, but one example can be drawn from Days 3, 4, and 7. On Days 3 and 4 the issue of microscope competency was introduced. The cheek cell biopsy on Day 7 incorporated a complete review of microscope use, and can be seen as a response to that earlier discussion. Consequently, from Taylor's point of view, he *had* attended to the issue of microscope competency in fairly concrete terms; that is likely why he was concerned about how much could be expected of the students and of him.

As Taylor suggested, the issue of the microscopes seems to reflect the underlying differences in his and Oliver's teaching styles and strategies — differences they both agreed needed to be discussed at some point. Given the syntax and tone of Oliver's feedback about microscope competency, it is not clear that his concerns directly resulted from concerns about context and continuity. The discussion went beyond the boundaries of context and continuity, and entered the realm of expectations. Instead of remaining with the specifics of how-many-students-did-what-with-the-microscopes, the central issue became the differences between Taylor's and Oliver's classroom expectations. In addition, the discussion tended to focus on the immediate past rather than on what could be done in the future.

Finally, given the substance and positive tone of the earlier part of the conference, there is a question of proportion. If a comment on microscope competency was warranted it might have been sufficient to reduce its proportion to something as brief as: "I noticed that a number of the microscopes were put back incorrectly and, given the concern about their care, maybe the students need to go over those rules again when you aren't so pressed for time. . . ."

Friday, Day 12

Co-operative Work

This episode shows the tension between getting students involved in microscope work and the inherent difficulties of that work. Oliver and Taylor co-operatively work toward a solution for future lessons.

Class

In this lesson students were to finish their drawings of normal and cancerous kidney tissue and proceed with observing and drawing liver and lung tissue. Taylor began by detailing his expectations for the drawings. He then contributed to the pedagogical context of the lesson by explaining why he had set up three microscopes at the back of the room with slides of normal, coal dust contaminated, and cancerous tissue:

265 **T** *The limitation . . . was the fact that I only have one single cancer slide, so what I did was I set up the microscope at the back, and in fact I have set up three. I have got all three lung slides there. Now, if you want to take a [normal] lung slide to your desk, you are welcome. . . .*

Taylor expressed his concern about the care of the microscopes, reviewed how they were to be handled, and announced that he would give marks for proper care.

266 **T** *Now another thing that I wanted to talk to you about before we start: I was a little disappointed yesterday to see the way that some people are handling the microscopes. . . . Mr. Brown, in the advanced level ten, is quite concerned about these microscopes, quite rightly so. He is responsible for the equipment and the facilities. He has got to look at how they are going to be repaired and replaced, and his class period one is using them as well. All the rules that I talked about as far as microscopes go, are not so that you have rules, [they are] so the microscopes are in OK shape. . . . However, I am a little bit worried about the swinging microscopes around and holding them above the shoulder and, you know, whipping them around the desks and stuff. . . . So, for your own sakes, and for me and Brown, and for the microscopes, I want you to exercise the kind of care I was talking about. Brown, by the way, gives ten marks for the microscope being back in the right place and away properly — you know, the cord wrapped around the neck, no slide left*

on it, all the parts there, cleaned off, on low power, the cover on it, back in the right space, OK? . . .

At the end of the exercise Taylor reiterated instructions for putting microscopes away:

267 **T**   *Please do not forget to put your microscope away in the prescribed manner. I am going to be marking that, remember? Low power. No slides left on it. Switch turned off. The cord wrapped around the neck. Cover on in the right spot. I would like you to put them away now. Time is running out. When you have your material away, give me back my pen, hand in the stuff, etc. Have a good long weekend, and see you Tuesday. The field trip. You have a period two class on Tuesday.*

Conference

Taylor indicated that he was not feeling great and that it was one of those days that he might have assigned relevant seat work were it not for wanting to maintain the continuity of the project. In spite of his misgivings, however, he felt that the lesson had gone well. Taylor raised the issue of the microscopes and Oliver mentioned that he had wondered if Taylor was uncomfortable talking to the students about them:

268 **O**   *I thought in my mind, "Is he uncomfortable talking about this?"*

269 **T**   *Not discomfort with the topic. I am feeling rough today. It is general discomfort, I think.*

270 **O**   *Fine, OK. You know, I thought you dealt with that well.*

271 **T**   *I didn't get enough sleep last night. I am feeling a little blah. I don't want sympathy, I am just trying to answer your question.*

Taylor went on to explain that the microscope issue was important to him, not only because of what happened in Thursday's class, the subsequent conference, and his own concern as a biologist about the care of the microscopes, but also because of a colleague's concern that they be treated in a certain way:

272 **T**   *You know, I am a biologist, I use them every year. I pull them out for the first time and I see what they are like after the other teachers have put them away, and so I know what it is like to be on the receiving end.*

273 **O**   *You mentioned that issue earlier.*

274 **T**   *Yeah, a lot of this is teacher stuff. It is important to me that Brown is not stressed by the fact that I am not controlling those microscopes. That is important to me as a teacher-teacher thing, and so I prefer to lay it onto these kids, although I am not being unreasonable with them, to make sure that that is preserved between Brown and me. It is important. [Later in the*

conversation] You said, "Why do they have to be on low power?" Remember, I answered, "Because Mr. Brown wants them on low power." I mean, I know why, it is because you start on low power, so when you get the microscope out it is already on the scanning power. But, I mean to me, the issue there is not, "They have got to be on low power for the person when they start." For me, the issue is they have to be on low power or Brown will be upset. Do you see what I am trying to say there?

The discussion turned to the issue of timing and the fact that students were not able to finish all of the drawing before the class was over. Taylor makes the point that a teacher does not want students left with nothing to do.

275 **T**   *Especially in general, if you are going to make a mistake, you want to make a mistake in that you have a little extra work and you ease up on them and you say, "That is OK, you have been working well." And they appreciate that. You don't want to be in a situation, especially with this kind of equipment out, where they start looking at the fingernails underneath the microscope because they are finished and, you know, pull their hairs out or, "Let's smash a slide." I really had hoped that they would get through it all. They really agonized over how they were going to draw it, which was a bit of a surprise to me.*

Oliver pointed out the difficulty students had seeing what they were intended to see. This is a common problem with microscope work and, again, concerns students' need for relevant context in order to known what they are to do and understand. Oliver talked about context in terms of "orienting" and providing an "organizer." The discussion moved between identifying problems and exploring potential solutions for future lessons. It is a good example of co-operative work:

276 **O**   *Yeah, I spent some time with Doug and David and some with Tom, and Brenda grabbed me and asked me a few questions. They get into the trap of — they are presented with a lot of material when they look at that slide. First of all they have trouble orienting themselves to know what is there. I mean I even have that trouble when I first look at it, and their problem is trying to determine what is a cell and how much one should draw. And when I went around the classroom some of them were concentrating on one or two cells and obviously listened to you very carefully and picked that up and they were fine. The other thing was . . . . Merle and David were up there and they were drawing whole piles of cells. They had thought that that pile of cells was in fact one cell with a bunch of little things in it, where it was multinucleated. And even spending some time with them there, I found that frustrating, initially, but they got on to it. And, thank God, in those microscopes we have pointers. . . .*

277 **T**   *This is an example that I wouldn't have thought of, if you hadn't been here. I just wouldn't have thought to have done it. It wasn't something that I didn't bother to do, or I forgot to do. It never occurred to me, and it is a fantastic idea. I know that, now that I think about it, I know that you do that because*

it is still in the microscopy work from the Classification Unit. But it never clicked to me that — with these kids, with the difficulties that they are having — that probably what would be really good for them would be to set up a day, a microscopy lab that is a demonstration lab with a dozen microscopes, and [have the students] move from one to the other. Well, I mean a dozen scopes, maybe not a dozen different specimens. There are three different specimens, and have them set up. Tell [the kids] not to move them. Use the good scopes, and put the pointer on something. Have a sketch beside it, and tell them to look and identify, draw and label.

278 **O**   Yeah, that would be nice. . . . You know, we expect them to know what a cell is and to be able to observe it and to distinguish cytoplasm, and the nucleus, and then you look in that slide and there is no organizer. . . . Brenda, for instance, when she looked in there, she thought that a whole group of cells — which I think was part of the glomerulus in the kidney, and I wasn't even sure to be quite frank with you — was in fact one cell with a bunch of little dots in it. After I carefully adjusted the focus you could see the cell membranes. I showed her that it was in fact a bunch of cells that happened to be round, and they were kind of pie shaped, and there was a dozen or so cells there. [She said], "Oh yeah, I can see that," and she was fine. So that it just needed that organizer at the beginning.

279 **T**   Which was basically what you and I did this period, [we went] around desk to desk — because you can't do it as a group. You can do it as a group, damn it. We have got that projector-microscope. You know, these ideas just come to you like this, and the frustration of it is, it comes to you like this normally. . . . But in the normal circumstance, by the time September rolls around you have forgotten again. You go through it and you miss it again.

280 **O**   What would be really neat for this program — it is something I hoped to get for this school a long time ago and we never were able to do it. Maybe we should push on it again with the advent of laser video disks, and the fact that we are going to be going to TV monitors in the classroom. I would love to have two monitors hung up at the front of this classroom and a projection camera that would sit on a microscope, like a TV camera, so that at the beginning of a class like this on microscopy, wump, you put a slide on there and you say, "Now, look, see, there it is. Now look in your microscopes."

281 **T**   We can do that now, before we get all that stuff. We could do it right now with that projector [and screen] . . . . And you hang up a piece of white Bristol board right beside the screen and you teach them how to draw. When are you going to teach them how to draw? When do they teach them how to draw?

282 **O**   Yeah, that is a fantastic idea.

Considerations

The end of this conference is a particularly fine example of one aspect of the feed-back process — an actual event in the present class was used as a basis for developing future plans for a unit of material and for teaching. The talk between Oliver and Taylor (276-282) was collegial and co-operative, and raised several significant points. For example, Oliver clearly identified an important issue of context — the need for an "organizer." Preparing students for what they are expected to see and do, and providing context establishes a frame within which students can place their work. Oliver's comments were specific, but not judgemental. And, significantly, he was *involved* in the incident itself; he did not play a strictly observational role. (Not all teaching situations allow for that kind of involvement, however.)

In addition, the "Considerations" of Day 9, which outlined personal and professional sources of stress for a teacher, were elaborated upon in this conference. Taylor emphasized the importance of maintaining good relationships with his colleagues. Few would deny the importance of that and, in situations where teachers are pressed for time to complete activities using shared equipment, it is easy to see how respecting a colleague's wishes is all the more significant. (Teachers of advanced-level courses sometimes assume priority with regard to expensive equipment and this can also contribute to professional tension.) Maintaining healthy collegial relationships is only one of a host of immediacies that leave little or no time for recording the day's events with a view to the future. As Taylor notes, ideas come into his head, on-the-spot, all the time (as they do for most teachers), but there is seldom the time or energy for attending to them and "by the time September rolls around you have forgotten again" (279).

Wednesday, Day 13

Stress of the Process

The hospital trip does not go as planned and as a result lacks continuity with the theme of cancer and cell biology. Taylor ties a film on lung cancer to earlier work with cilia. Oliver raises a question about "evidence" but does not tie it to the focus on context and continuity. The process itself contributes to stress.

Class

Monday was a holiday and Tuesday was the hospital trip. There were no student project reports on this Wednesday. Taylor began by discussing the trip which had not worked out as expected. His class was included with several other groups on a general tour and his students did not get to see anything with regard to cancer diagnosis or treatment. In spite of this, he complimented students on how well they behaved (although some did not attend) and solicited their reactions:

283 **T** *Boring, what did you mean by boring? Be honest because I want to run this trip again. I want to know how to make it not boring. Come on Ralph, John, come on. I want to hear what you have to say.*

284 **S** *It was so complicated, like, the stuff they were talking about.*

285 **S** *It was too educated.*

286 **S** *Yeah, nothing exciting about it, you know. Talk about something you have never heard of, you know. . . .*

287 **T** *I got the feeling that they were talking from where they were at with their university education without understanding that they were talking [to high school students]. You couldn't understand what they were talking about and that makes it boring. Was that the kind of thing that was a problem? It wasn't being there that was boring, it was the way they were talking to you so . . . I think that is something that we can change. . . .*

Taylor then introduced a film on smoking and its relationship to lung disease. He began by setting the context:

288 **T**   *We have been talking about cancer and cells for a long time. I want to stop talking about cells. We are going to look at something on a little higher level, and just to remind you — I think you have got this in your book already so you don't have to write this down — you have been looking at the cell. Inside the cell are cell parts which we called organelles. OK? We looked at a specific one, right? We looked at the nucleus, and the rest we just called cytoplasm. We looked at the cell membrane. We looked at the cell, we talked about cancer — Bill, are you trying to tell me that there is no safe place in the room?*

289 **S**   *He is still bugging me for a coke, sir. I don't have any money.*

290 **T**   *We looked at cancerous and normal cells and compared this. . . . A group of cells with the same function are called tissues. The little sacs where the air exchanges with the blood, the alveoli, are tissues — a bunch of cells with the same function. The lung contains several tissues: blood vessels, the alveoli, air tubes, muscles, connective tissue, etc., and it is called an organ, OK? We are going to look at it today and a little bit tomorrow at this level, the tissue level, the organ level. And since we have been talking about the lung, I want to continue to talk about the lung. We are going to talk about the obvious thing, the major thing. I was reading an article today which was about how to lie with statistics so I am going to bite my tongue and I am not going to tell you what percentage of people die of cancer because they smoke, but it is the major, overwhelmingly the major, cause of lung cancer. So if we talk about lung cancer, we have to talk about smoking. How many people in here smoke? Come on?*

291 **S**   *Come on, Ralph!*

292 **S**   *I know, but I quit.*

293 **T**   [Later] *Now I want your attention. For those of you that don't smoke, I think it is very important that you not turn off. This is not meant to be a campaign to stop smokers. What this is meant to be is for you to understand the difference between one's health when one smokes and one's health when one doesn't smoke, and you can be on either side of that fence. So don't turn off because this is about smoking and you don't smoke. Maybe you need some good feedback as to what a good job you are doing for yourself.*

When the film stated that smokers cough to get rid of dirty air in their lungs, Taylor interrupted to make a point about evidence. During the ensuing discussion the following occurred:

294 **T**   *Just a second. Let's deal with this and then I will answer your question, OK? How does your body move stuff out of the lungs or out of the windpipe or out of your nose?*

295 **S**   *There is something — a tube.*

296 **T**   *Yeah, the dirt collects in the tube. How does the dirt get out of the tube? We haven't talked about this very long but remember the cilia that I talked about, that we were hoping to see with the paramecia? We talked about the fact that the hairs and mucus, yeah, the mucus traps it. That is the filter you are talking about. . . .*

Later the film made reference to the cilia: "Human lungs are very delicate. The breathing tubes are lined with small hairs called cilia." As the film rolled, Taylor interjected:

297 **T**   *Ah hah, here are the hairs I was talking about. . . . I said that we were going to look at them under the microscope. You couldn't see them. I told you they were there, and now I am showing you an animation.*

   After the film, Taylor provided reading and worksheets on respiration and breathing which were to be completed as homework. Taylor asked the students to bring cigarettes for the following day's lab with smoking machines at which time they would also discuss cures for cancer. He announced that on Friday there would be a test on cancer and that he would introduce their next unit on astronomy.

Conference

This was the last day that Oliver observed Taylor's class, and the last formal conference between the two. At the start both talked about how the hospital trip could be made more relevant to the unit (Oliver had attended and helped supervise the class). One idea that emerged was to bring in an expert on cancer from the hospital or the Cancer Society to talk with the class. From there Oliver and Taylor's discussion turned to the issue of timing (Taylor had a second film which he did not have time to show), and Taylor linked the issue to his agitation at the beginning of class:

298 **T**   *I had a very serious interaction with the front office seconds before the class. You [probably noticed] I was obviously very agitated in the class, but I managed to settle myself down. . . . Perhaps it will make sense to talk about that later.*

299 **O**   *I think you used the field trip discussion just to try and calm yourself down.*

300 **T**   *That is exactly what I did. I was very agitated. That is the context. As far as the lesson went — I wrote out another lesson plan for you, it is upstairs, I will make sure you get a photocopy of it — to try and organize myself for the end.*

301 **O**   *You are providing context and continuity and closure.*

302 **T**   *Yeah, I have two films. One I showed today, "Smoking is Your Choice." The other one is "Smokers' Lungs." It is a little more appropriate for what we are doing. The two together I think are important so I figured, of course,*

"Smoking Is Your Choice" at the beginning, the worksheets in the middle, and the other film at the end. Well, of course, once we took up the field trip — you go into class and if the lesson goes well ... you stop and talk about the stuff. You notice how, as an alternative to the first movie of this unit where they had a question sheet, we talked about the movie all the way through.

303 **O**   I liked that. I liked the way you dealt with evidence too. You know, you discussed the evidence of the film and that we were trying to push on what is good evidence.

As they talked about the use of evidence, Oliver commented on those occasions when Taylor tried to highlight the importance of having evidence to back up scientific claims while, at the same time, he appealed to higher authority. That led to speculation about how Taylor might handle the issue the next time he taught the unit:

304 **O**   You are appealing to higher authority. . . . A number of times you said, "I read this, I read that," but if the students push you on that one and say, "What is the evidence that you are really referring to?" then you would have to go back. . . .

305 **T**   Yet I am coming from a totally different angle. What I am doing is I am saying, "Here is the evidence. Now, take that for what it is worth. It is just words. Because remember I held up that magazine, the one of the two headed boy in the jungle. You read that, too, but that doesn't make it a fact. I read it. In a way what I am trying to say is I am not telling you what the truth is. I am telling you what I read." However, you are right. It may in fact be misconstrued as a higher authority. . . .

306 **O**   Yeah, because you see, when you talk about reading articles — and, of course, you give them something like that newspaper article — and when you are talking about reading, they may have difficulty distinguishing, that is all.

307 **T**   We are going back, maybe at the beginning of the course, as part of my whole introduction — because I am going to save that "two headed boy" article; I may even make photocopies of it, and use that at the same time as the "evidence" film at the beginning of the course. And then compare it to say a good example, a good but a simple example, of a research paper. And then later on in the course when I say something like that off the top of my head, maybe they will have a better feeling for it. That is exactly what I want. Anyway, the intent is skepticism. That is good.

In a previous conference Oliver indicated that there were students that Taylor seldom interacted with during class time. In this conference he returned to the issue:

308 **O**   I think I like what you were doing today. You were pushing on the students who — you were consciously pushing on those kids that you don't talk to.

309 **T**   I talked to Jane today, and Steve.

310 **O**   *That is right. That is one of the good pieces of feedback from this program. And you talked to Hugh at the end. And you had some discussion with Sally and Doug — yeah, a number of times with Doug. . . . I like the way you did that. Let's see, anything else that you [want to discuss]?*

Taylor mentioned his satisfaction with how he had handled the homework assignment. Earlier in the case, he had expressed concern that the unit did not have homework already integrated into its format. Oliver had pointed out at that point that Taylor could develop and assign homework if he wished.

Finally, in the context of his perception and concern about bringing the unit prematurely to a close (because of the end of Oliver's formal involvement in the project), Taylor provided further insight into how he would like to work with a unit of material:

311 **T**   *I keep feeling like I have a deadline. In fact I can see, without your having been here, I could have seen this running on and only having a few days at the end [of school]. So what I will do is a little bit of astronomy, like the space program. And, in fact, remember I commented that I wanted two weeks for astronomy — now I have four. I think probably if I was able to do everything I wanted, I would have two.*

312 **O**   *Fair enough. Obviously what has to be thought about for next year is how much time you do want to devote, what resources are you really going to use and what you aren't going to use. You have introduced a whole new set of resources, which is this package.*

313 **T**   *But that is normal. . . . The limitation of this program is it forces you to solidify a unit of work before you start, and I never ever taught that way. . . . [For example], look at what I picked up in the middle of the unit — so it goes another day. The priority in the past for me, and probably for you, has been the flexibility. . . .*

Considerations

The hospital trip is a reminder that things sometimes do not go as planned. Oliver and Taylor had hoped the trip would emphasize the role cell biology plays in cancer diagnosis, but the hospital had other things in mind. The excursion turned out to be a general tour along with other student groups. Ironically, then, the experience became the kind of *discontinuity* that both the design of the unit, and Oliver and Taylor had intended to avoid (167–169).

During the conference Oliver brought up two issues not transparently related to context and continuity. The first was the use of "evidence," and the second concerned Taylor's involvement with students he generally did not interact with (308–310). Although both of these issues are related to context and continuity, the relation is not obvious and warrants spelling out in the conference. Remarks which are not explicitly tied to the issues of context and continuity, such as Oliver's compliments of Taylor's interaction with various students (310), run the risk of projecting the message that Oliver will comment on whatever he wants, and not adhere to the boundaries of the agreed upon focus. This is easier for a teacher to take when the comment is a compliment, of course, but in the end it does add to the persistent threat of the observer falling into a supervisory role.

An ongoing issue in the case study, this time raised by Taylor, was the stress that is part and parcel of a teacher's work. Stress can result from working with various colleagues, difficult students, the general working environment, and personal issues. In this conference Taylor attributes stress to several issues, including his interaction with the office (298–300). Although we are not privy to the substance of that interaction, it is a reminder that the act of teaching itself is often a very delicate matter, one that requires intense concentration if it is to be done well, and one which is potentially affected by a variety of factors in a teacher's life.

Other points of stress concern the unit and the feedback process. Taylor obviously feels constrained by the timetable of the unit and, although it was not part of the agreement that he end the unit when Oliver left, he feels pressured to do so (311–313). Such pressures are somewhat indefinable for Taylor, but relate to the fact that the whole feedback process was construed within the parameters of a "project." It is entirely understandable that a teacher (like many people) might find being observed stressful, but in this case the documentation of both the classes and of the conferences contributed to that stress. Taylor emphasized this point some time later when talking with me about the case.

One of the themes running through this entire account concerns the precarious nature of the feedback process. The process itself can be very stressful. The history of feedback (regardless of the euphemisms) is laced with superficiality and insincerity; it is a history that does not bode well for trusting and honest interaction, in spite of good intentions. The historical context is such that both the teacher and the observer are often fighting an uphill battle to make the process fulfill their espoused goals. Nuances of interaction that might be insignificant in a different context can have severe consequences for the "collegiality" of a well-intended feedback process. For example, when the boundaries of discussion are not made clear or followed, the possibility that feedback will veer from its collegial intent and degenerate to an "old style supervision," increases the stress for the teacher.

Finally, the broader context of the case study should not be forgotten. This was a draft unit, a trial. It was Taylor's first time teaching the unit and, as with any first run, it was not expected to go entirely smoothly. In fact, the history of implementation suggests that it is normal for things to *not* go smoothly, which is partly why an argument can be made for constructive feedback. As MacDonald has pointed out,

> Incompetent pupils, incompetent teachers. Incompetent project? Not necessarily. Genuine innovation begets incompetence. It deskills teacher and pupil alike, suppressing acquired competencies and demanding the development of new ones. . . . In the end the discomfort will be resolved one way or the other, by reversion to previous practice or by achieving new skills, and new frameworks. But the discomfort and dismay are built in; they are defining characteristics of innovation. . . .[1]

The experience of teaching a draft unit for the first time is inherently stressful; it must be understood and respected as such by Oliver as he gives feedback to Taylor, and by us as we reflect on the account.

---

1. Barry MacDonald, "Innovation and Incompetence," in *Towards Judgement: The Publications of the Evaluation Unit of the Humanities Curriculum Project 1970–1972,* ed. Donald Hamingson (Norwich: Centre for Applied Research in Education, Occasional Publications No. 1, 1973), pp. 89-92. Quoted in L. Stenhouse, *An Introduction to Curriculum Development and Research* (London: Heineman, 1975), p. 170.

Reflections

Oliver and Taylor made a number of remarks about the feedback process during the experience and, later, in reflection. Here my interpretations of their feelings set the stage for my own reflections about feedback. Several points emerged in the various interviews I had with each participant over the course of the project. For instance, Taylor found the concepts of "context" and "continuity" useful reference points when looking at intellectual issues in the classroom. The whole process forced him to focus on a variety of issues that he might have paid less attention to under other circumstances. He felt that the experience would likely affect how he would handle this unit of material in the future. The process also seemed to provide a stabilizing influence during difficult periods. Some of this was because the demands of the project could not be ignored and consequently focussed his attention away from other personal and professional concerns. But some was due to the strong supportive role played by Oliver at critical points. In fact one of the more positive aspects of the process for Taylor concerned the opportunity that it gave him and Oliver to work on their professional relationship.

Oliver echoed the importance of the process from an interpersonal and professional standpoint, and in a later conversation with me noted that both he and Taylor thought that the personal aspect of the case should be highlighted in the account. Their professional relationship had not always been as comfortable as they would have liked. My sense is that they both felt that they had been through an intense process and each had emerged with integrity and a feeling that the process had been substantively and interpersonally constructive. Oliver thought that he had come to understand Taylor much better as a person and was more understanding and less critical of his teaching style. He was also positive about his own involvement in the project because of the opportunity it gave him to think about staff development within the science department. The experience helped him remember the complexities of teaching general-level courses. Although he had observed many classrooms, this was the first time that he had observed day-to-day activity for an extended period of time.[1] The process provoked him to think more intensely about the internal consistency of individual courses and the continuity of the whole program, and it contributed to his resolve to work more closely with his teachers upon his return to the department. Oliver thought that Taylor had become increasingly aware of issues like intellectual continuity and had attended to them appropriately while teaching the cancer and cell biology unit.

Both Taylor and Oliver were circumspect about less positive aspects of the process. My interpretation is that they were somewhat overwhelmed by the amount of time taken from their daily routines. Taylor found the conferences worthwhile, but the daily forty-five to sixty minute sessions stole time from his other activities within the school. And, although the work involved professional development, he was not released from other duties and obligations. Taylor also sometimes found the process intrusive because of its infringement on his established routines and habits which normally allowed him to cope with demands on his time and energy. This intruisiveness of the process became a source of stress in his daily life. Some of the stress resulted from the project making him look at issues that a teacher may not find easy to face (a paraphrase of a comment by Taylor during an interview). But some was due to the implicit pressure to teach in ways not always congruent with his usual approach.

Oliver found the feedback process draining because of its intensity and because of the uncertainty it provoked. For example, he frequently wrestled with the question of how hard to push on any particular issue with Taylor. At other times he wondered about the extent to which he should be drawn into Taylor's personal life and was concerned about whether he had the necessary skills to get personally involved, even when it seemed warranted. Finally, some of his frustration was due to his perception that, at times, progress seemed slow.

Images of progress

A theme throughout this account is the complexity of the feedback process and the sense in which it is an art learned throughout a professional career. Its complexity has been embedded in the detail and considerations throughout the case. Several issues of complexity, however, are less transparent, if no less significant, and can be used to tie together some of the interpretive strands of the account. For example, Oliver's apparent frustration about pace and progress is not an insignificant matter — it speaks to his image of what success with the process might look like.

In retrospect, at various points tension emerged from the different guidelines used by Oliver and Taylor to judge progress with the process. Taylor tended to use a past and future-referenced criterion: "This class is going better than in previous years; this feedback is useful for what I might do next year." Oliver's tendency was to use a present-referenced criterion: "Here's what this lesson could have been." Underlying the two orientations is a question of the extent to which *change* should be a criterion of progress and, if so, how much change should there be, how soon should it happen, what should its nature be, and what should be regarded as evidence for it. The tensions provoked by these questions are not necessarily counterproductive; nor were they always present in the interaction between Taylor and Oliver, as is clear from the details of the account. But articulating the context surrounding such questions can help explain why tensions emerged in this case with regard to "progress," and why these kinds of tensions may be predictable in many feedback situations.

The atmosphere of Oliver's professional working context, for example, was saturated with the rhetoric of change. "Change," "improvement," "accountability," and "excellence" were frequently overheard terms that kept administrative life in the fast lane. The school system as a whole was energetic and took an aggressive stance toward many complex issues. It represented a demographically fluid and culturally diverse population, and there seemed to be a common attitude that change was urgently needed but was almost always too slow in coming.

In my view, the working atmosphere and frenetic pace within central administration was especially exhausting for the more conscientious, like Oliver. As a highly qualified "special-projects" officer, Oliver was a trouble-shooter, implementation guide, resource person, and workshop presenter, to name a few of his various duties. These duties were only modestly reduced during the project with Taylor; the hard driving world of central administration was still part of his daily routine. The fast pace and rhetoric of change in this world would not easily be set aside when moving to a more reflective, observational role. It is not hard to imagine, therefore, that an observer might be frustrated if a teacher's rate of change seemed, at times, slow.

The context surrounding Taylor's professional life was quite different. It was also fast paced, but the pace was set by the number, frequency, and intensity of everyday teaching events rather than a drive for change. Thinking of Taylor's situation in terms of organic homeostasis sheds light on how he managed the multiple demands on his time. He avoided counterproductive stress by maintaining a dynamic equilibrium between his personal and professional worlds. Routines and habits assisted in establishing and maintaining a delicate balance among competing demands on his loyalties and time. At any instant his actions were often the result of an intuitive weighing of these demands. But these actions, in turn, set new conditions which had to be taken into account without upsetting the balance Taylor had established. The homeostatic metaphor lends understanding to his argument that, as a result of meeting daily with Oliver, it had taken time to establish a new rhythm in his daily routine (257). It can also shed light on how an apparently simple issue like bringing the unit to a close was complicated by a variety of factors that had to be considered: the integrity of the subject matter, the spirit of the unit, the needs of the students, the perceived demands of the project, and Taylor's concern with how to fill the time to the end of the school year (311).

In this homeostatic view, a teacher's daily life is a series of microadjustments, in which an acceptable balance is struck among many factors in the professional environment. Seldom is any one factor resolved as fully as a teacher might like. There are trade offs. For example, one issue that runs through this account is the difficulty of working with students like Steve. This was a source of concern for Taylor; and yet, stressful as the issue might have been, for a variety of reasons (time of year, past history, his personality, etc.) Taylor decided not to confront it as a major item on his agenda. In spite of how stressful a chronic situation might be, the integrated context might be such that to establish a new dynamic equilibrium would be more stressful than to maintain an established equilibrium.

Within the organic metaphor, changes in teaching, when warranted, may come relatively slowly. It takes time to establish a new dynamic equilibrium. When Taylor speaks of the value of feedback in terms of what it means for his work in the following year (279), he is taking into account the time it would take to assimilate the information and contemplate the possible consequences of what he might do. Of course it will not take a full year to accomplish that, but it is not a process he can engage immediately; currently his energies are devoted to teaching and absorbing feedback, and later his concentration will be on teaching other material. The next opportunity to focus on the issue will be in a year's time when he teaches the unit again. This unavoidable time lapse highlights the importance of documenting what happened, and of sketching alternatives for the future. These records are essential for remembering significant details. Unfortunately a teacher often does not have the time which the documentation process itself requires.

As a teacher himself, Oliver recognizes that, to some extent, immediate and visible change is an inappropriate criterion of progress in the feedback process. His concern about "how hard to push" can be interpreted as reflecting a quandry about the extent to which change should be a criterion of progress with the process. But if immediate and visible change is not a criterion of progress, what is?

Here it is important to articulate what is implicit in this day-by-day account. Both Taylor and Oliver put an incredible amount of time and energy into the two week process. Because of their sustained and intense involvement, each had to regard himself as a potent force in the process in order to carry it through. The commitment of time and energy would not be tolerable if either man saw himself as ineffectual. For Taylor a considerable portion of this case was devoted to uncovering the demanding professional world he lives in; it is a world of constant interaction with students, peers, and administration, a world in which a dynamic balance has to be struck between the persistent demands of the classroom and all the other professional obligations.

Oliver's role was no less demanding, if for different reasons, and it is accurate to say that he was exhausted by the process. If an observer is to maintain the committed involvement that Oliver did, it is likely that he or she requires tangible evidence of the result of that hard work. Such evidence is frequently conceived in terms of teacher change. But from the teacher's perspective there are any number of situations in which change may not be warranted immediately, if at all. A teacher might recognize the significance of feedback but need time to imagine its consequences for current practice. And it does not strain the imagination to suppose that as the insights about classroom phenomena become more profound, the likelihoood that *immediate change* in teaching practice is either warranted or possible decreases.

The interpretation I am constructing here involves tensions for Oliver (not uncommon in feedback situations) and contradictions in his account of Taylor's progress. On the one hand, as I have outlined, Oliver was at times frustrated by Taylor's seemingly slow progress in implementing the central concepts of the feedback process; this can be related to his image of what constitutes an acceptable rate of "change." On the other hand, on several occasions he expressed the view that Taylor understood central concepts (like context and continuity) and was dealing with them appropriately in the classroom situation. This would seem inconsistent but, in the complexity of the situation over time, both of these images were realities for Oliver. At times, one image was more dominant than the other, at other times both "feelings" coexisted as compartmentalized realities.[2] Because of the luxury of systematic reflection over the entire account, we can see that Taylor attended in one way or another to nearly every item of feedback brought forward; but it is likely that, embedded in the immediacy of the situation, Oliver was not critically aware of that, focussing instead, perhaps, on the rate at which Taylor was able to do what was appropriate *without* feedback. Different images of progress with the process (involving change and rates of change) give rise to the apparent contradiction between Oliver's feelings and Taylor's behaviour.

An observer requires some criterion to monitor how well the feedback process seems to be going. Where change in practice is an inappropriate measure, the level of *sincerity* is one criterion that can be used. On those occasions when change might be anticipated but is not evident, an observer likely will be sensitive to whether or not the teacher seems to be taking the process seriously. The observer tacitly will be integrating a variety of clues to sincerity — nuances of the conversation, consistencies, inconsistencies, non-verbal information, and the like.

Sincerity is a matter of perception, of course. Those perceptions (well or ill founded as they may be in a given instance) help set the tone for the whole feedback process. In the preceding case study, for example, the incidents of Day 3 (use of a plant cell with the microscope when it had been previously agreed that only the paramecium cell would be used) and Day 6 (Taylor forgot to ask Oliver to bring the prepared slides to class) could lead Oliver to question the extent to which Taylor was engaging the process seriously. If that were the case, it could help to explain the kind of mentor-student relationship that occasionally surfaced in the feedback process (characterized by feedback which went beyond the bounds of the issues of context and continuity).

Sincerity is significant to both parties, naturally. The teacher has no less desire to be heard and taken seriously. A considerable part of the interaction in this case study can be seen as Taylor's attempt to bring Oliver to a fuller understanding of context influential in shaping the events of his teaching life. Thus Taylor was sensitive as to whether the complexity of his world was taken seriously. Taylor seemed to interpret Oliver's concrete support (both personal and professional) as affirming that Oliver took him seriously as a teacher and as a person.[3]

The possibility of different images of progress is a factor which contributes to the complexity of the feedback process and to its quality as an ongoing learning experience. One of the reasons giving constructive feedback is an art learned over a professional lifetime is because facility with the process depends to a large extent on building a repertoire of skills and understandings that come from constant and cogent reflection on rich cases of practice. In this particular case different images of progress is one of the issues that Oliver will likely grapple with as he works and grows with the process. Other cases will have other issues, all of which will be integrated with the substance and interaction of the feedback process.

Learning the art

Learning the art of constructive feedback is difficult, time consuming, and an ongoing process. The art derives its character from two broad features: responsiveness to changing nuances of new situations; and recognizing the "integratedness" of different issues within the process. The former aspect favours fluid, dynamic visions of the process over those which emphasize form and mechanics. The latter involves identifying significant issues, not only about teaching, but about the process itself, and integrating these issues with each other and with the particulars of a given situation. There are many significant issues that serve as a backdrop to any given instance of feedback practice, of course. These typically contain tensions that require active and ongoing resolution. Differing images of progress with the process, discussed above, is one example.

Three other issues also illustrate some of the complexities of the process. First, it is important that both the teacher and observer have a clear understanding of who is responsible for what. The teacher's responsibility is to the students. *It is the teacher who has responsibility for what happens in a classroom, not the person giving feedback.* It is the teacher who must weigh alternative strategies, plot courses of action, intuitively respond to immediacies, and existentially accept responsibility for the conduct of classroom life if not for the personal learning of each child. It is the teacher's responsibility to weigh the feedback and take it seriously; to do otherwise would be to make a sham of the process. It is not the teacher's responsibility to uncritically accept advice about what to do.

The observer's responsibility is to the teacher. It is the observer's responsibility to give feedback which is constructive, but not to accept personal responsibility for what happens in the classroom. When the observer begins to have a (misplaced) sense of responsibility to the students, she or he is likely to begin to worry when the teacher does not do as the observer would have done. It is the observer's responsibility to communicate the results of her or his analysis to the teacher in the clearest and most helpful way possible. The observer's role is not to give advice that must be followed.

These points may seem obvious, but in real situations the distinctions between roles are not easy to maintain (which is why the question of "whose problem is it?" is the focus of attention in so many therapeutic and interpersonal situations). Not accepting responsibility for the students does not mean that the observer can ignore the students' interests. In fact, the observer's and teacher's analyses of events in the classroom miss the mark if students are not a focus. Part of the observer's analysis needs to include a sincere effort to understand events from the student's point of view; this is difficult to do without at the same time assuming a measure of responsibility for the students. Another reason the locus of responsibility is hard to maintain is that good, heartfelt feedback requires that the observer also view a situation from a teacher's point of view. Initially at least, it is through the observer's own experience of teaching that she or he is able to connect with an observed situation. The observer tends to imagine what she or he might have done in the situation as a teacher. This is probably a natural and vital part of the process and may help avoid an unhealthy detachment. But those same images tend to carry with them the (also natural) feelings of responsibility to the students; it is here that the process can begin to part ways with what we might expect from genuine collegiality.[4]

A second issue concerns the observer's breadth of understanding of both the nature of the subject matter and of teaching. In short, an observer benefits from a fund of pedagogical "know-how," much of which is learned through experience. Oliver, like any teacher, needs to have more than subject matter knowledge. His knowledge of biology must be integrated with his understanding of teaching — he may have insights, for example, about what issues can be problematic for students. He must combine his knowledge of students and classroom situations with what he knows about the subject matter and, at the same time, consider pedagogical issues.[5] Oliver must go into the feedback situation with these issues clear in his own mind while maintaining an attitude which respects different points of view.

Third, it should be recognized that constructive feedback involves the integration of essential skills which are spiritually at odds with one another. Oliver must learn the skills of tough analysis: he must bring his subject matter knowledge and pedagogical knowledge to bear on the fine details of specific teaching situations. At the same time he needs to hone an entirely different set of skills — those of empathy, understanding and listening. In short, the hard-nosed analytical skills must be tempered with an equally important set of "counselling" skills. The ability to appropriately integrate these two types of skills in a given situation is a continuously learned art because no two situations are identical.

Learning the art of constructive feedback is, like teaching, a constant process of trying and trying again. It entails reflecting on situations, having conversations about them, building a repertoire of skills and understandings, taking into account past instances but remaining sensitive to unique qualities of new instances, not getting rigid and stale, and trying again. The terms "learning" and "art" suggest a particular attitude toward the feedback process and allude to its distinctive features. The process is referred to as an art because, although particular skills are fundamental, elegant practice of the process goes beyond skill. Feedback, when well done, is not mechanical and, even though it requires a kind of thoughtful planning, it relies on intuitive judgement. Such judgement is responsive to the moment — responsive to nuances and unanticipated changes, as well as to the meaning of the predicted routine — and appropriately and simultaneously takes into account numerous features of process and substance. Practitioners who are "artful" with feedback can be distinguished from those who seem to have all the right skills and can produce them on demand but may practice in a wooden or mechanical or stilted manner.

However, feedback *is* learned; a practitioner can become more skilled and more artful with increased understanding of the nature of the process and with reflective practice. The phrase "learning the art" is a way of signalling that it is a continuous learning process. Learning must involve an attitude of inquiry about instances of real practice. As with any qualitative inquiry, it is a matter of systematically analysing and interpreting the data of the feedback process. It involves trying things out, making judgements, formulating and testing hypotheses, making predictions, and developing explanations about the phenomena of feedback (and of teaching) with a view to developing an increased understanding and more artful practice. Workshops, seminars, courses, training sessions, and so on are all ways of getting new ideas and acquiring or honing skills; but, although they should be engaged throughout a career, they alone will not render a practitioner artful with the process. The development of artfulness requires that the practitioner constantly monitor her or his practice and treat it as a matter of inquiry.[6]

Time, place, and concepts

Implicit in these reflections and in the entire case study is the notion that constructive feedback in teaching is itself a reflective process. Reflection can lack potency in the absence of a relatively rich set of concepts which can be brought to bear on a situation — the absence of richness limits the potential of reflection on that situation, and limits the avenues of appropriate action.[7] Some concepts may emerge from the data — that is, there are occasions in which the details of a situation are such that one is provoked to look at it in a different light. However, more commonly, concepts are brought to the situation and constitute the lenses through which the situation is seen.

Concepts which can be used to address important issues in teaching need to go beyond mere technique. Concepts like "continuity," "context," and "reasons" have this potential, but they are only a few among many. However significant a concept may be, it must be pedagogically meaningful enough to be useful to a teacher who is actively working on the relationship between abstract concepts and the particulars of practice.

Reflection also requires an appropriate setting and, while this case study of Oliver and Taylor's interaction documents one such setting, many others are imaginable and would probably be required, given current institutional constraints. The constraints of setting are clear in Taylor's case. Taylor was in charge of all the general-level science courses in his school, which meant that none of his science colleagues had similar teaching situations. His setting inhibited the kind of conversation with colleagues which might be conducive to mutual inquiry and reflection.

Oliver emphasized several points related to setting. He felt that if boards of education truly wanted "excellence" in the classroom, then teachers would have to have more time to work with each other. Teachers need time to build the kinds of relationships that might foster constructive feedback, and time to deal concretely with issues of substance. He noted, for example, that there was a push for teachers to deal with science and society issues, but that many had little background about these issues to guide their curriculum development and classroom teaching.

Oliver also stressed how important it was for him to have someone to talk to as he worked through the process with Taylor. (I was that person in this particular case.) My view is that Oliver did not want advice, but neither did he want to be working in a vacuum, talking to himself. Just as a teacher may from time-to-time want someone to talk to about teaching, so too does an observer want to talk about giving feedback. Oliver needed someone with whom he could organize his thoughts and run through his thinking on a matter. Having someone to talk with helped him maintain a reflective, inquiring attitude toward the process.

Reflective processes like constructive feedback on teaching take *time*. It is appropriate to end with an observation about the time required of both the teacher and the observer if they are to seriously engage in a reflective process. *I think it would be hard to over emphasize the centrality of the issue of time.* The feedback process can become self-defeating when teachers are not given time to pause and reflect. Surely this is one of the aspects of the phenomenon of "burnout." As a poignant example, upon returning to the classroom and to his formal duties as department head, Oliver was persuaded by senior administration to continue a major commitment to his "special project" duties. He was expected to do that without any reduction in his teaching load or departmental duties. Consequently the demands on Oliver's time were such that he was unable to follow through with his intention to spend more observational time in the classroom. He had intended to work on teaching and curriculum development with his teachers (some of whom had expressed interest as a result of his work with Taylor), and to reflect on his own growth in the feedback process. One of the ways that talk about reflection and feedback can become rhetoric is when the time and resources it would take to seriously engage the process are severely underestimated. It is a sad commentary on educational priorities and the pace of professional life when two teachers must scrounge for time to observe and systematically reflect on teaching. As Erickson states:

> Teachers in public schools have not been asked, as part of their job description, to reflect on their own practice, to deepen their conceptions of it, and to communicate their insights to others. As the teaching role is currently defined in schools there are external limits on the capacity of a teacher to reflect critically on his or her own practice. There is neither time available, nor an institutionalized audience for such reflection. The lack of these opportunities is indicative of the relative powerlessness of the profession outside the walls of the classroom.[8]

And yet there is evidence that the time is ripe for serious attention to the reflective aspect of teaching. A recent position paper on teacher education in Ontario emphasizes the importance of a period of induction for beginning teachers which, through reduced work load, would provide a "structured opportunity for practice, reflection and discussion, [and a] *chance to observe and be observed by experienced colleagues*."⁹ It is not hard to imagine learning the art of constructive feedback as an integral part of teaching careers. Oliver and Taylor's work together is an important beginning for them both, and is a valuable contribution to the general understanding of the feedback process.

---

1. This point needs to be emphasized, but it should *not* reflect poorly on Oliver. Few people, except for a relatively small handful of researchers, have spent observational time in classrooms on a continuous basis — that is, day after day for an extended period of time. Consequently, all manner of issues concerning rhythm and habit in the classroom (like intellectual continuity over time) may go unnoticed, *except by the students who must face them every day*. Both Oliver and Taylor were sensitive to this fact and it is to their credit that they were willing to participate in a project in which that was taken into account.

2. Thomas Green provides an illuminating discussion of the logical and psychological structure of beliefs in his "A Topology of the Teaching Concept," in *Concepts of Teaching: Philosophical Essays*, ed. C. J. B. Macmillan and T. W. Nelson (Chicago: Rand-McNally & Co., 1968), pp. 28–62.

3. It is important to note that issues of genuine interaction and sincerity are important to both adults and children (see the discussion concerning "Interpersonal reasons," p. 9).

4. The distinction concerning the locus of responsibility has some rather far reaching consequences in at least two areas. The first relates to the relationship between teacher evaluation and professional development. I have serious questions about the extent to which feedback under the flag of evaluation (formal or informal, formative or summative) can attain a high degree of collegiality simply because in the final analysis evaluators do have some formal responsibility to the students. (This is not to say that some evaluation procedures are not more enlightened than others or that a teacher may not "develop" as a result of having been evaluated.) By extension, I wonder to what extent it is actually possible for those giving feedback to wear an evaluation-hat on one occasion and a colleague-hat on another. (Which is not to say that progress has not been made in recent years in this area; school boards are beginning to show an increasing sensitivity to these kinds of issues.) The second area concerns structural aspects of the observer's role. There are indications that feedback works best when there is an element of genuine reciprocity. Even in Oliver and Taylor's case, things tended to go more smoothly when both were actively involved in the class rather than Oliver being a passive observer. Active participation in classroom life may be one indicator of a productive feedback situation. It is not hard to imagine situations where both participants might have ownership of the teaching situation (although not necessarily at the same time). Team-teaching is an example of a kind of classroom relationship in which both parties would at different times and in different ways play a participant-observer role — sometimes taking the lead as inquirer, sometimes as teacher, but never as teacher without maintaining some attitude of inquiry. On the face of it, team-teaching would seem to present an optimal setting for rich and constructive feedback that could inform both the teaching and feedback processes. Here again, however, it would be important that each teacher develop an intuitive sense of when his or her responsibility was to the student and when it was to the colleague.

5. For a discussion of the relationship between pedagogical understanding and subject matter knowledge, see: B. Kilbourn, "Reflecting on Vignettes of Teaching," in *Reflection and Teacher Education*, ed. G. Erickson and P. Grimmett (New York: Teachers College Press, 1988), pp. 91-111. Also see B. Kilbourn, "Situational Analysis of Teaching in Clinical Supervision," in *Learning About Teaching Through Clinical Supervision*, ed. W. J. Smyth (London: Croom Helm Ltd., 1986), pp. 111-136.

6. Donald Schön's *The Reflective Practitioner* (New York: Basic Books, 1983) is helpful for understanding what inquiry means in practical situations like teaching. For example, with regard to "hypothesis-testing," he argues that:

The inquirer's relation to this situation is *transactional*. He [or she] shapes the situation, but in conversation with it, so that his own models and appreciations are also shaped by the situation. The phenomena that he seeks to understand are partly of his own making; he is *in* the situation that he seeks to understand.

This is another way of saying that the action by which he tests his hypothesis is also a move by which he tries to effect a desired change in the situation, and a probe by which he explores it. He understands the situation by trying to change it, and considers the resulting changes not as a defect of experimental method but as the essence of its success. [pp. 150-151]

Also see, D. A. Roberts and A. M. MacKinnon, "Reasons for Giving Reasons: An Expert-Expert Clinical Analysis of Science Teaching for Non-Academic Students," *International Journal of Qualitative Studies in Education,* in press. And, A. M. MacKinnon, "Detecting Reflection in Action Among Preservice Elementary Science Teachers," *Teaching and Teacher Education* 3(2), (1987): 135–145.

7. The term "reflection" has gained popular use partly through Schön's work (see note 6 above). The term has a place in discussions of practice because of its common-sense meaning — thinking seriously about practice. This common-sense meaning excludes (a) rule-bound behaviour which ignores attention to the nuances of specific situations, and (b) rationalized behaviour which courts self-serving, unconsidered justification of actions. In most human situations as complex as teaching (and feedback on teaching) there is a fluid tension between reflective and rationalized practice.

8. F. Erickson, "Qualitative Methods in Research on Teaching," in *Handbook of Research on Teaching,* ed. M. S. Wittrock, 3rd ed. (New York: MacMillan Inc., 1986), p. 157.

9. M. Fullan and F. M. Connelly, *Teacher Education in Ontario: Current Practice and Options for the Future* (Ontario: Ministry of Colleges and Universities, 1987), p. 36 (my emphasis).

Questions and Responses

During the construction of this case study I received feedback from many people who were teachers in one capacity or another. Some were university teachers in the field of education. Many were primary and secondary school teachers, some with little experience, others were department heads or consultants with ten to twenty years teaching experience. Some had backgrounds in science teaching but many did not — English teachers, math teachers, social studies teachers, a pre-school teacher, a professor of social work. Many of these people were in graduate courses at the time they gave me feedback on "Constructive Feedback." Some were in a course which emphasized reflection on one's own teaching; others were in a course which addressed the process of feedback; still others were in a course which focussed on methodological issues in interpretive research. These courses were run as practica and involved students in reflecting on the nature of the messiness of live situations.

The feedback I received was enormously helpful. Much of it pointed to areas where I had not been clear or where the reader needed more help in order to see what I had intended. Some did not point me to do anything, but indicated that the case was connecting with the professional lives and concerns of real practitioners. But some of the feedback I received needed to be addressed directly; it could not be handled by taking away from or adding on to the body of the account. Consequently, I wish to respond to the following questions from readers as part of the spirit of inquiry that should permeate discussions about teaching and about feedback on teaching:

Questions about the Case

(1)   What was your (Kilbourn's) role when Oliver and Taylor were working together? (p. 110)

(2)   Could you elaborate on what you mean by the term "construction"? Is the case made up? (p. 111)

(3)   Can you generalize from one case? (p. 112)

(4)   You assume that a single case "can contribute to an understanding and improvement of future practice" (p. 18). How might that work? (p. 112)

(5)   Why is there so much data in the account? (p. 113)

(6)   Would you prescribe this kind of feedback for practitioners in schools? (p.113)

(7)   What was constructive for Taylor? (p. 114)

(8)   You suggest that a change in *teaching* should not be a significant criterion of progress with the feedback process and argue for sincerity as a benchmark. But what about the possibility of expecting a more immediate change in the way a teacher *thinks* about practice? Wouldn't change in how a teacher *thinks* about practice be a reasonable criterion of progress with the feedback process? (p. 115)

(9)   What about the power differential between Oliver and Taylor — wouldn't the outcomes have been different if they had been on a more equal footing? Shouldn't teachers be equals if they are to give feedback to one another? (p. 115)

(10)   For a constructive feedback process shouldn't the participants be willing? What can be done about the unwilling participant? (p. 116)

(11)   How much training is required before a person can give constructive feedback? (p. 117)

(12)   Are you implicitly saying that the approach represented by giving reasons and supplying context and continuity is the approach that should be taken when teachers give feedback to one another? (p. 117)

(13)   How important, really, is the idea of giving reasons? Does it make a difference to students or do they regard reasons as just more reified mumbo-jumbo? (p. 118)

(1)   What was your (Kilbourn's) role when Oliver and Taylor were working together?

I was not present during their work but intermittently had separate interviews with them (see pp. 15-16). My approach was to seek descriptive clarification about what had been happening in the feedback process and to acquire a sense of the meaning and importance ascribed to events by each participant. In retrospect, the interviews served two functions. One, outlined above (p. 106),was to be a sounding board for Oliver as he worked through the process. My role was not to give advice, but rather was to assist Oliver by listening and clarifying various situations as he worked through the process as an inquiry. The other function was to construct the account. The transcribed interviews were the starting point for putting the case together. They allowed me to focus on those aspects of the process that were significant to each participant. It was through studying the interviews that I was able to construct a sketch of the entire case from beginning to end. Each day's account was constructed by moving among the interviews, Oliver's field notes, and the transcribed conferences between Oliver and Taylor (the primary data source).

(2)   Could you elaborate on what you mean by the term "construction"? Is the case made up?

Nothing was made up — the things that were said were actually said (and on tape) and the things that were done were actually done (as documented and reported by Oliver and Taylor). There was a high degree of coherence among what was said between Oliver and Taylor, my interviews with each of them, and the notes taken by Oliver.

The term "construction" refers to issues of selection and interpretation. It relates to my desire to tell a particular kind of story and tell it in a particular way. Many things were happening in this account and part of my project was to show that very point — to show the complexity of the feedback process. Because of the complexity, any number of stories could have been told. For example, a story could have been told which emphasized the curriculum development and implementation aspect of the case. One could have been told which emphasized teaching technique, or which emphasized the institutional setting within which teaching occurs. Another could have been told which emphasized the personal aspect; another could have focussed on the role of the subject matter in teaching. Still another story could have been constructed around the methodological, interpretive, and ethical issues in the case. In each of these alternative stories, different threads and themes would have been brought to the forefront while others would have stayed in the background or receded from view altogether. Each, if emphasized, would have required a different presentation and, in some cases, a different approach to inquiry. Throughout the account what I have included in the "Class" and "Conference" sections, and written about in the "Considerations," has been governed, yes, by the "reality" of what happened, but also by an intent to say something to practitioners about one of the stories — about feedback and the context within which it is conducted.

While the feedback story is not made up, it is, nevertheless, constructed. The construction of the published case-as-read comes from having to select from enormous amounts of information — a file drawer full of transcriptions, notes, notes about notes, and all the artifacts of qualitative inquiry in progress. Selections and interpretations for this mass of data had to be made in order to tell a coherent story about feedback. For instance, Oliver and Taylor were very articulate and had little trouble conveying their thoughts and emotions. However, listening to a tape or reading a verbatim transcript of their conversation is difficult. One minute Taylor is talking about management, in the next breath he is talking about something personal, and then he adds a point that is not general but is particular, referring to Steve, all in the context of trying to explain to Oliver a pedagogical event that might have lasted less than a minute. In the middle of this Oliver may interject with a phrase which is simply a reminder of an entire conversation held on a prior occasion.

Making the transition from spoken conversation to written dialogue poses a difficulty. On the one hand, I wanted to respect what Taylor and Oliver were saying and the way they were saying it (which is why the bulk of the account consists of their transcribed conversations). They were articulating the several levels of reality that run simultaneously in any event; the half-sentences, unspoken words, emphatic phrases, and pregnant pauses were part and parcel of their way of using language to convey the integratedness of things, the phenomenology of events. I did not want to lose this; as outlined in the "Foreground" to the case, conveying the integrated nature of events was one of the tasks of the account.

And yet, to leave the conversation of Oliver and Taylor in its unadulterated state would be so distracting (and so lengthy) that a reader would lose patience and the point. Consequently, selections were made. Careful attention was paid to the meaning of what Oliver and Taylor were saying as I sorted through their conversations looking for sections which said something about context and continuity in teaching, and about substance and interaction in feedback. I did not emphasize issues that were mentioned by Oliver and Taylor but of little apparent import to them (this involves a judgement on my part and a leap of faith on the part of the reader which is an issue in any interpretive account). Nor did I include information that might breach explicit or tacit ethical commitments. And deletions were made where something significant was frequently repeated but in different ways. In this way the account was "constructed" so that in prose it would have, to some degree, the same "seamless" quality that the events had in real life. My intent was to illustrate the complexities of a process in a way anticipated to be informative to those concerned with feedback in teaching. The *construction* of the case study was shaped by my image of its function.

(3)   Can you generalize from one case?

I do not want to review here the lengthy discussion about "generalizability" of case studies.[1] But to take the question at face value the answer would be "No." Strictly speaking none of the events in this case study will be repeated (or repeated in the same way) in another case even if it involved Oliver and Taylor. Usually, however, we are not interested in such "strict" generalizability. More pertinent questions are ones like, "In new instances, will there be feedback issues of substance and technique that will have to be addressed?" Or, "Will future cases exhibit ups and downs like Oliver and Taylor experienced?" The answer to these kinds of questions is "Yes, most likely" or "Quite possibly." My graduate course on feedback involves students in a practicum situation in which they reflect on the feedback they have given a teacher in a genuine teaching situation. Experience with this course over a ten year period suggests that the issues with which Oliver and Taylor were involved were not at all atypical in a general sense, even though they were unique in a specific sense.

It seems to me that the question of "generalizability" must be addressed within the context of how people learn about practical work, and within the related context of the function of a case study like this one. The intent is not to make general claims about a population of colleagues giving feedback. *Its function is to provoke reflection about feedback by taking the reader through an actual instance of its practice.* It is a teaching-learning function and assumes that one of the ways we learn about practice is by reflecting on realistic accounts of it (sometimes our own and sometimes those of others). Each new case contributes to our repertoire of understandings and skills for dealing with future cases. Within this context, generalizability of specifics is not required; but, given the intent, if insights from the case were not thought to be in some sense relevant to future instances, there would be no point in telling the story.

(4)   You assume that a single case "can contribute to an understanding and improvement of future practice" (p. 18). How might that work?

The relationship between an instance of practice and a practitioner's thoughts about future practice is complex and will vary from practitioner to practitioner. Nevertheless, there are several commonly recognized ways in which case studies contribute to practice. Highly descriptive accounts of pratice allow a reader to put him or herself in the place of those in the account. Such cases stimulate thinking by allowing practitioners to see themselves as others might. At other times, while the abstract concepts used to characterize episodes of practice may be familiar to the practitioner, the value of an account is that it shows how these concepts relate to the particulars of practice. The question, "What counts as an instance of X?" is addressed and allows the teacher and observer to see, for example, what is meant by "conceptual continuity" or "overload." The account can assist the practitioner to see the degree to which his or her situation exemplifies the case in point.

In other cases, an account may provide ideas as to what may be *done*. Insofar as actions or reactions to a situation can become habitual, past experience influences a person's sense of what is reasonable to do. An account can provide vicarious experience which can expand (or limit) the scope of a practitioner's reflecting and acting.[2] In still other cases, the function of an account is to look at the familiar from a different point of view, usually with the hope of bringing fresh insights to commonplace, and sometimes stale, images of pratice. The intent is to contribute to the understanding of practical situations by proposing alternative ways of thinking about them. These various functions are not mutually exclusive, of course, and a given account may fulfill different functions for different practitioners. This case with Oliver and Taylor provides one of many possible instances of practice upon which to reflect.

(5)   Why is there so much data in the account?

I take this question as asking why the account is so long and why there is so much quoted material from Oliver and Taylor. The reflective, teaching-learning function of the case requires that *particulars* be explicated within their context as much as is feasible. For example, it is helpful for a practitioner who is trying to learn the process of feedback to see what might count as an instance of, say, "overload" (Day 2). Or, it is helpful to understand a particular instance of how events at a later stage of the process might be seen to be affected by the subtleties of earlier events. Particulars in a context give a practitioner more to reflect on than do abstract generalities; and they take time and space to explicate. Within this general point I had several related agendas: on behalf of the subject matter, it was important to document an entire unit of material so that issues about its integrity could be articulated; on behalf of students, I wanted to construct an account which at least gave some sense of events over time; on behalf of teachers, I wanted to construct an account that allowed them to speak rather than one which encapsulated what they said and did. All of these agendas pointed toward a lengthy rather than abbreviated account.

(6)   Would you prescribe this kind of feedback for practitioners in schools?

Yes and no. It depends on what is meant by "this kind of feedback." On the whole I would argue that teachers should give feedback to one another as a routine part of their professional growth. They should do so in circumstances in which they genuinely want to engage the process. Further, they should treat the data of teaching (and of the feedback process itself) as an inquiry. These would be the only relatively unqualified prescriptions I would be inclined to make about feedback.

My experience of listening to teachers suggests that they do want to talk about their teaching in more than superficialities and that they welcome constructive feed-back as part of that discussion. But the opportunity to engage in discussions of actual practice is limited. As frequently remarked, a teacher's professional life is lonely in spite of the fact that it entails being immersed in a sea of human interaction day after day. Given this picture, it is not at all unreasonable to suggest that a significant step in the profession would be for teachers to be able to expect high quality feedback from one another when they want it. What constitutes high quality or constructive feedback is an issue for inquiry, not for rhetoric; but at the very least it is something other than insensitive criticism or gratuitous praise.

Collegial discussion about teaching will likely be more fruitful if it is conducted with an inquiring attitude since that is a powerful way of avoiding hyperbole, moralizing, and unrealistic expectations. Continued monitoring and learning about feedback needs to be built into the process itself. Again, one way of contributing to that learning process is by reflecting on instances of actual practice. The Oliver and Taylor story is one of those instances. Its function is not to prescribe that teachers "do likewise," but rather to provide those who are interested in the feedback process with an instance to think about.

As to the question of prescription and the particulars of Oliver and Taylor's work together, their situation, like any other, had dozens of qualities that gave it a unique character. None of these qualities could be reasonably prescribed for another setting without qualification. For instance, Oliver and Taylor worked with the feedback process for thirteen consecutive days — the duration of the unit of material being taught. After the fact we might inquire as to whether that was the best plan, would we do it that way if it were to be done again, what was learned at what price, and so on. Clearly, it would be foolish to suggest that all feedback be of such duration and intensity. And yet, in some circumstances that might be quite appropriate. A central question is, given a specific situation, what approach makes sense for a teacher and his or her colleague, and how can it be carried out elegantly, with rigor and dignity, and to the satisfaction of all participants? The only general prescription would be that teachers should engage in active inquiry about their teaching through constructive feedback (but not only through that, of course), and that they should treat the process itself as a matter of ongoing learning.

(7)   What was constructive for Taylor?

There is no simple answer to this for Taylor or for any practitioner. Some aspects of the process were more helpful than others for Taylor, as is evident from the details and analysis of the account. Participants probably need to aim for an active and open discussion *about* the feedback process as it unfolds since this allows the teacher to more easily voice what he or she finds constructive. Sometimes Oliver and Taylor were able to do this, and sometimes not. It should be recognized, of course, that a participant's feelings about a complex process like feedback are likely to be equally complex and that there may be more to the issue of "what is constructive" than an immediate verbal response. An awkward or uncomfortable exchange about a sensitive issue may seem unconstructive at the moment to a teacher but, over the course of time, may come to be seen as important and helpful. Conversely, feedback can be thought at the moment to be constructive, but later may be regarded as less so (because it did not deal with relevant particulars, or glossed over important issues, and so on).

At times Taylor did explicitly say that a particular bit of feedback was helpful. While he never said that it was unconstructive at any particular point, we might infer from his expressed frustration and acknowledged stress that at times it was. And yet, in spite of the frustration, he always dealt with issues brought up by Oliver. One interpretation of this is that he was intimidated by Oliver and, consequently, was just doing what he was (implicitly) told to do. (I personally do not find that interpretation plausible; the evidence does not point to Taylor as an automaton.) An alternative interpretation is that, in spite of what he might have felt and said at any given moment, Taylor attended to the substance of feedback because he did find it constructive, given the uncertainties of the unit of material he was using. Which of these (and other) interpretations is more reasonable is not the question at this point; rather, what could Oliver have done at the time, if anything, to enhance the constructiveness of his feedback? The entire case is about that issue and, as we read the case, it can be seen that the question, "What is constructive?" is not only complex, but cannot be addressed without reference to both the teacher *and the students*. Furthermore, the question cannot be answered in the abstract; it is, once again, an issue for practical, ongoing inquiry about particulars — at every step of the way "what is constructive" needs to be addressed by the participants.

(8)   *You suggest that a change in teaching should not be a significant criterion of progress with the feedback process and argue for sincerity as a benchmark. But what about the possibility of expecting a more immediate change in the way a teacher* thinks *about practice. Wouldn't change in how a teacher* thinks *about practice be a reasonable criterion of progress with the feedback process?*[3]

Criteria of progress with feedback will vary from case to case. A change in practice and how a teacher thinks about practice would normally be regarded as evidence that the process is taken seriously. But I want to take into account those cases where a teacher seriously engages the process even though practice or ways of thinking are not immediately changed — perhaps a slow evolutionary process begins which culminates in a different attitude towards practice some time in the future. In such a case the process could be regarded as successful even though there might be little immediate evidence of change in the way a teacher thinks about practice. I would argue that *sincerity* is a necessary condition for the process to be considered successful, and that a teacher can take the process seriously without changing thinking or practice. In many cases perhaps some evidence of change in the way the teacher thought about practice would be anticipated. And, obviously, in some instances it would not be unreasonable to expect some change in practice. But it is also possible to have successful feedback which changes neither thinking nor practice, as when a teacher solicits and receives outside corroboration for the characterization of a teaching situation, or for why some aspect of practice works well.

(9)   *What about the power differential between Oliver and Taylor — wouldn't the outcomes have been different if they had been on a more equal footing? Shouldn't teachers be equals if they are to give feedback to one another?*

There is little question that unequal power can complicate the feedback process; and yes, the case probably would have looked different had Oliver not been Taylor's department head. (The reverse is also true; inexperienced teachers tend to have a difficult time giving feedback to their seniors.) The power difference is easy to identify in Oliver and Taylor's case. In the abstract it is easy to imagine a situation where a power difference would not pertain, but teachers who are equals may not be as common as one might think. In most cases there are too many sociological nuances in the relationship to expect issues of power not to be a potential factor. This is why the feedback process must rest on something other than authority, why it should be conceived as inquiry, as a discussion about the data of teaching in which hypotheses about teaching and learning rest on evidence, argument, and perspective rather than on authority. Issues of authority and power can get in the way and are among the many challenges to constructive feedback processes.

But in many cases a differential in expertise is associated with a differential in status and power. For example, the idea of "mentoring" (one kind of relationship in which constructive feedback might be used) assumes a differential between the two participants. The mentor is generally expected to have more experience and to have something to teach; his or her expertise lies in being *an* authority rather than *in* authority.[4] The nature of the relationship is such that it is the responsibility of the mentor to demonstrate the reasons why he or she is *an* authority. Without "reasons" the relationship runs the risk of degenerating to one in which the neophyte teacher perceives the mentor as *in* authority; here issues of power can become problematic.[5]

It should also be recognized that consultants, department heads, vice-principals, and principals frequently have responsibilities for the professional development of teachers which may, from time to time, involve feedback. These people usually are perceived as having more "power" than the teacher, but, at the present at least, they are among the few in a school who have the kind of control over their time that is needed to practice feedback. The challenge for these people is to learn how to avoid the misuse of power. Treating the feedback process as an inquiry provides a setting for the participants to explicitly address the question of power. Circumstances in which two teachers work collaboratively (mentoring and team teaching, for example) is a goal to aim for; but if feedback is limited to only those who are perceived to be "equals" in an effort to avoid issues of power, we risk choking the possibility of feedback becoming an integral part of ongoing professional development.

(10) For a constructive feedback process shouldn't the participants be willing? What can be done about the unwilling participant?

I am concerned about the role of feedback in the ongoing professional development of a teacher. One criterion in an image of an ideal setting for truly constructive feedback is that the teacher *wants feedback* on her or his practice. This is more than just "willingness." The participants must intend to seriously engage the process. (And that process may or may not be carried out under a variety of additionally supportive conditions — team teaching, co-operative research, reciprocal feedback, and so on). The basic argument is straight forward: when a teacher wants feedback she or he should be able to get it and it should be of high quality — it should be constructive for both the teacher and the students. But the willingness (even eagerness) of the participants is not enough for feedback to be constructive even if additional supportive conditions, like reciprocity, are in place. It will be of little use if you and I engage in a process of reciprocal feedback, but one or the other or both of us continues to do it poorly. That will only reinforce latent suspicions that the process is painful and of little help. We must both be active and sincere learners and inquirers of the feedback process, and we must teach ourselves to become sensitive to the kinds of issues to which Oliver and Taylor were becoming sensitive.

Oliver and Taylor *were* willing participants. As I think back to the early discussions with them, prior to the case, it would be fair to describe them as enthusiastic. However, as should be clear, there were a number of features about the setting that were less than optimum. While both Taylor and Oliver were quite willing, they were not the instigators of the process. While Taylor agreed with the general focus of the feedback, he did not initiate the process. And, too, it is artificial to have the whole process documented as part of a project. All of this is to say that, in a variety of ways, Oliver and Taylor's circumstances fell short of an ideal setting. But that is why the case is important; few actual situations will meet our visions of the ideal, but they can still help us learn the process.

Finally, it should be clear that I am not talking about situations where someone in authority perceives that a teacher could benefit from feedback and the teacher is going to get it whether she or he wants it or not. I am talking about how we learn to be constructive with feedback so that we will look forward to getting it when we want and we will begin to see its use as an integral part of our development as teachers.

(11) How much training is required before a person can give constructive feedback?

I am ambivalent about this question because of its phrasing and the term "training." How long it takes to become "constructive" obviously will depend on the individual. Undoubtedly there are experiences that a person can go through which will contribute to learning the feedback process. Courses, seminars, training sessions, and repeated practice all are likely to be helpful in this regard. Generally speaking, formal experiences (like courses) that concern counselling and interaction and those that concern curriculum, teaching, the nature of learners, and the nature of the subject matter will all be relevant. But the reason I refer to constructive feedback as an art learned over a professional lifetime is that it is not simply a matter of training. It is not a matter of going through a finite number of seminars or workshops or courses and coming out at the end "trained."[6]

I believe that the real issue is whether or not an introspective and inquiring attitude is brought to bear on experience in the classroom and in the feedback process (including a healthy dose of scepticism for razzamatazz and platitudes). Formal experiences like courses have their place, but what is more important is that an inquiring attitude toward feedback be fostered — that the question, "What is constructive in this particular situation and to whom?" not fade from the attention of participants.

(12) Are you implicitly saying that the approach represented by giving reasons and supplying context and continuity is the approach that should be taken when teachers give feedback to one another?

No, there is no necessary connection between the substantive approach taken in this particular case and the feedback process in general, which is not to belittle the importance of reasons, context, and continuity to students' learning. While every feedback process is guided in part by points of view (sometimes articulated, sometimes not; sometimes trivial, sometimes not), those views need not relate to issues of "reasons." We can readily imagine feedback in which other points of view framed and guided the process. It depends on the situation. There are several reasons for the point of view guiding the present case.

The central reason relates to the past history of the project and the nature of the unit of material itself. As indicated earlier, the curriculum materials were constructed with an aim to make connections, have continuity, provide reasons, and so on. Early observations indicated that a lot would have to be done in the act of teaching for those kinds of connections and links to be made. These empirical considerations set the stage for "reasons" being the substantive focus in Oliver and Taylor's work. Beyond that, I wanted to provide an example of a focus that was non-trivial, one that would have some "staying power" over the long term as one useful way of looking at aspects of teaching.

There obviously could be considerable dispute about what is and is not a non-trivial point of view on teaching. But I wanted to move away from standpoints that emphasized only technical issues. For example, it is not hard to imagine a focus that would address the "activity" aspect of working with students who do not relate well to school. Here the argument might be that because these students are often restless they should be engaged in doing rather than passive sitting. Empirically that may well be the case, but it is limited as a framework for feedback unless it is set within the broader context of *meaning*. Why? Because we can readily imagine a classroom where students are pacified with activities but learn little because the activities are disconnected, fragmented, and bear little or no relationship to each other. In the end a sole focus on "activities" would beg for a distinction between teaching and entertaining — which is not to say that teaching should never be entertaining, but that we typically expect more from teaching than entertainment.[7]

I also wanted to show an instance of a substantive approach being *sustained* over a period of time so that learners of the process could see in some detail what it looks like to maintain a focus in a feedback process. At the same time the case illustrates what it looks like to drift from the focus, and provides an opportunity to "play" with the grey areas and hypothesize what might have worked better and why some things worked well.

(13)   How important, really, is the idea of giving reasons? Does it make a difference to students or do they regard reasons as just more reified mumbo-jumbo?

The question, as phrased, speaks to issues of efficiency, but my response also has a moral component. The efficient argument assumes that issues like context and continuity are important if there is reason to believe that attention to them will help the child learn more or learn faster or like learning more. But testing these beliefs would be empirically difficult and hard to interpret. For some students it probably will be mumbo-jumbo, for others it will not. At the level of common sense it seems reasonable to suggest that students will do better in school and like school better and will drop out less if they are able to understand more easily that which they are expected to learn. And it also seems common sense that they will find understanding easier if "reasons" are central to the classroom in appropriate ways at appropriate times. The efficient question is important and should not be dismissed.

But, as stated before, "giving reasons" is not a panacea. The question, at least as worded, is somewhat cynical because it suggests that in the absence of obvious success we should abandon the effort. (At its worst it hints that schools are such alienating places that nothing we do could possibly make a difference and I regard such a stance as defeating to students and teachers alike.) The efficient slant of the question focusses attention away from important moral issues. Much of what we do in the classroom is done for moral reasons. We teach in certain ways because to do otherwise would simply appear to us to be morally wrong.[8] Giving reasons in the classroom strikes a tone which is in keeping with much of what we espouse as educationally important in a democratic society (critical thinking, problem solving, intellectual independence, and the like). It is morally incumbent upon us to respect the role of reasons in the classroom because they are integrally linked to broader ideas of an educative process.[9] Consequently, we may teach in ways that respect the role of reasons, continuity, and context in the classroom even though at all points along the way we may not have demonstrable evidence of immediate (efficient) outcomes.

---

1. As a starting point see, for example: Robert Donmoyer, "The Rescue from Relativism: Two Failed Attempts and an Alternative Strategy," *Educational Researcher* 14(10), (December 1985): 13-20, or Frederick Erickson, "Qualitative Methods in Research on Teaching," or Robert Stake, "The Case Study Method in Social Inquiry," *Educational Researcher* 7(2), (February 1987): 5-8.

2. Donald Schön provides an interesting discussion of the function of *imitation* in guiding practice. See his *Educating the Reflective Practitioner* (San Francisco: Jossey-Bass, 1987).

3. This question is complementary to Question 7. Here the question tends to assume the observer's perspective rather than the teacher's.

4. R. S. Peters makes this distinction in *Ethics and Education* (London: George Allen and Unwin, 1966).

5. See D. A. Roberts and A. M. MacKinnon, "Reasons for Giving Reasons."

6. For example, Oliver had taken a course on clinical supervision five years prior to his work with Taylor. He had also participated in leadership seminars and workshops on interaction. The course involved thoroughly analyzing two instances of his own feedback behaviour and met for two and one-half hours a week for thirteen weeks. These training experiences would be considerably more extensive than what most teachers attempting to work with the feedback process would have had, yet even Oliver would be reluctant to say he had been "trained." (Taylor had been given feedback on several occasions, but to my knowledge he has attended no formal workshops or courses concerning feedback.

7. For discussions on the relationship between teaching and related activities see Paul Hirst, "What is Teaching?" *Journal of Curriculum Studies* 3(1), (May 1971): 5-18; and Paul Komisar, "Teaching: Act and Enterprise," in *Concepts of Teaching: Philosophical Essays*, ed. C. J. B, Macmillan and T. W. Nelson (Chicago: Rand-McNally & Co., 1968), pp. 63-88.

8. Scheffler refers to this as the "manner" in which teaching is conducted. See his "The Concept of Teaching."

9. Israel Scheffler argues this point in "Philosophical Models of Teaching," *Harvard Educational Review* 35 (Spring 1965): 131-143.

Bibliography

Barnes, D. *From Communication to Curriculum.* Harmondsworth: Penguin Books Ltd., 1976.

Blumer, H. "What is Wrong With Social Theory?" *American Sociological Review* 19 (1954): 7.

Donmoyer, R. "The Rescue from Relativism: Two Failed Attempts and an Alternative Strategy." *Educational Researcher* 14(10), (December 1985): 13–20.

Erickson, F. "Qualitative Methods in Research on Teaching." In *Handbook of Research on Teaching,* edited by M. C. Wittrock. 3rd ed. New York: MacMillan Inc., 1986.

Fullan, M. and Connelly, F. M. *Teacher Education in Ontario: Current Practice and Options for the Future.* Toronto: Ministry of Colleges and Universities, 1987.

Geddis, A. "Perspectives on Knowledge in the Classroom: A Case Study in Science Teaching." Ed.D. dissertation, University of Toronto, 1985.

Goldhammer, R. *Clinical Supervision.* 1st ed. New York: Holt, Rinehart and Winston, 1969.

Green, T. "A Topology of the Teaching Concept." In *Concepts of Teaching: Philosophical Essays,* edited by C. J. B. Macmillan and T. W. Nelson. Chicago: Rand-McNally & Co., 1968.

Hirst, P. "What is Teaching?" *Journal of Curriculum Studies* 3(1), (May 1971): 5–18.

Kilbourn, B. "Situational Analysis of Teaching in Clinical Supervision." In *Learning About Teaching Through Clinical Supervision,* edited by W. J. Smyth. London: Croom Helm Ltd., 1986.

———. "Reflecting on Vignettes of Teaching." In *Reflection and Teacher Education,* edited by G. Erickson and P. Grimmett. New York: Teachers College Press, 1988.

Kilbourn, B. and Roberts, D. A. "Science, Society and the Non-Academic Student: Phase I." Final Report. Ottawa: Social Sciences and Humanities Research Council, 1983.

———. "Science, Society, and the Non-Academic Student: Phase II." Final Report. Ottawa: Social Sciences and Humanities Research Council, 1987.

Komisar, P. "Teaching: Act and Enterprise." In *Concepts of Teaching: Philosophical Essays,* edited by C. J. B. Macmillan and T. W. Nelson. Chicago: Rand-McNally & Co., 1968.

MacDonald, B. "Innovation and Incompetence." In *Towards Judgement: The Publications of the Evaluation Unit of the Humanities Curriculum Project 1970-1972* edited by D. Hamingson. Norwich: Centre for Applied Research in Education Occasional Publications 1 (1973): 89–92.

MacKinnon, A. M. "Detecting Reflection in Action Among Preservice Elementary Science Teachers." *Teaching and Teacher Education* 3(2), (1987): 135–145.

Peters, R. S. *Ethics and Education.* London: George Allen and Unwin Ltd., 1966.

Roberts, D. A. "Developing the Concept of 'Curriculum Emphases' in Science Education." *Science Education* 66(2), (1982): 243–260.

Roberts, D. A. and MacKinnon, A. M. "Reasons for Giving Reasons: An Expert–Expert Clinical Analysis of Science Teaching for Non-Academic Students." *International Journal of Qualitative Studies in Education,* in press.

Russell, T. "Analyzing Arguments in Science Classroom Discourse: Can Teachers' Questions Distort Scientific Authority?" *Journal of Research in Science Teaching* 20(1), (1983): 27–45.

Scheffler, I. "Philosophical Models of Teaching." *Harvard Educational Review* 35 (Spring 1965): 131–143.

———. "The Concept of Teaching." In *Concepts of Teaching: Philosophical Essays*, edited by C. J. B. Macmillan and T. W. Nelson. Chicago: Rand-McNally & Co., 1968.

Schön, D. *Reflective Practitioner.* New York: Basic Books, 1983.

———. *Educating the Reflective Practitioner.* San Francisco: Jossey-Bass, 1987.

Shulman, L. "Paradigms and Research Programs in the Study of Teaching: A Contemporary Perspective." In *Handbook of Research on Teaching*, edited by M. C. Wittrock. 3rd ed. New York: MacMillan Inc., 1986.

Simon, R. "What Schools Can Do: Designing Programs for Work Education That Challenge the Wisdom of Experience." *Journal of Education* 169(3), (1987): 101–116.

Smyth, W. J., ed. *Learning About Teaching Through Clinical Supervision.* London: Croom Helm Ltd., 1986.

Stake, R. "The Case Study Method in Social Inquiry." *Educational Researcher* 7(2), (February 1978): 5–8.

Stenhouse, L. *An Introduction to Curriculum Development and Research.* London: Heineman, 1975.